THE
Machu Picchu
GUIDEBOOK

A Self-Guided Tour

REVISED EDITION

Ruth M. Wright
Alfredo Valencia Zegarra

Johnson Books
BOULDER

Published by Johnson Books, a division of Johnson Publishing Company, 1880 South 57th Court, Boulder, Colorado 80301. E-mail: books@jpcolorado.com www.johnsonbooks.com

9 8 7 6 5 4 3 2

Cover design by Debra B. Topping
Cover photograph by Kurt Loptien
Artist Robert Guisti's rendition of Machu Picchu courtesy of
    National Geographic Maps

Library of Congress Cataloging-in-Publication Data
Wright, Ruth M.
    The Machu Picchu guidebook: a self-guided tour/Ruth M. Wright,
Alfredo Valencia Zegarra.—Rev. ed.
        p. cm.
Includes bibliographical references and index.
    ISBN 1-55566-327-3
    1. Machu Picchu Site (Peru)—Guidebooks. 2. Inca
architecture—Guidebooks. 3. Incas—Antiquities—Guidebooks. 4.
Peru—Antiquities—Guidebooks. I. Valencia Zegarra, Alfredo. II. Title.
F3429.1.M3W75 2004
918.5'37—dc22   2003023721

Printed in the United States by
Johnson Printing
1880 South 57th Court
Boulder, Colorado 80301

Contents

Machu Picchu foldout map follows page 190

Travel Tips

Getting There

It is always a little risky to give specific travel details because of the great potential for change. Therefore, a blanket warning is issued here: Always get the latest, up-to-date information when making your travel plans.

Most travelers to Peru land in either Lima or La Paz and take a flight to Cusco, the pre-Columbian capital of the Inca empire. The airlines from Lima are Aero Continente, LANSPERU, TACA and TANS. From La Paz the one airline is Lloyd. Flights to and from Cusco are in the morning when the temperature is lower and the weather is more dependable. The flight takes about an hour and may afford magnificent views of the Andes.

A note on travel arrangements. If you have limited time, we recommend making your travel plans and reservations in advance. If you want a Peruvian travel agency, which may be more familiar with the local scene, you can search the Internet for Peruvian firms. For example: http://www.yahoo.com; then enter Peru Tour Operators in the Search box; then click on Tour Operators for a list. From there you can go to their individual on-line web sites. Be sure any agency you pick is at least a member of the IATA (International Association of Travel Agencies), insuring minimum standards of quality. Travel books on Peru also usually list travel information. It is best to use e-mail or Fax to communicate with Peruvian entities.

From Cusco you will take a train to Machu Picchu—actually to Aguas Calientes at the base of Machu Picchu. All trains depart from the San Pedro station, opposite the central market. Most tourists take the comfortable Vistadome, which departs at 6:00 A.M. (06:00). Your ticket gives you a reserved seat in a specific coach. The round-trip price is about $90. In addition, a cheaper and somewhat slower train, with no reserved seats, the Turismo Economico (also called the Backpacker), leaves at 6:15 A.M. (06:15) with a round-trip price of about $55. (By the time you use this book, the prices may be higher and the departure times may have changed. Always check.) You may also travel by bus or car to Ollantaytambo, about halfway, and take the train from there through the Urubamba River canyon. There is no road through the canyon. The trip to Aguas Calientes from Cusco takes about three-and-a-quarter hours. In either case, get your train tickets early (at least several days in advance) so that your travel plans are not thwarted. If you know the dates you plan to visit Machu Picchu, order the tickets through your travel agent.

A recent addition to the train service is the very expensive Hiram Bingham at a round-trip price of about $360. It requires a short trip from Cusco to Poroy (a little station close to Cusco). It leaves at 9:00 A.M. (09:00) and returns to Poroy at 10:00 P.M. (22:00). Service includes brunch on board, a bus ride up and down to Machu Picchu from Puente Ruinas (the old railroad station that is somewhat closer to Machu Picchu than Aguas Calientes), entrance fee, guide, and afternoon tea and sandwich at the Sanctuary Lodge. The return trip includes dinner on board, with wine and dessert. (If you are interested in this option, be sure to check the details, that is, is it seasonal, is it still running.)

At Aguas Calientes you will board a bus just a short walk from the train station. Bus tickets can be purchased right where the buses are lined up, and a bus will leave as soon as it is full. After a spectacular fifteen-minute ride up the slope to Machu Picchu, the bus drops you off in the parking lot in front of the Sanctuary Lodge, an expensive but highly desirable hotel. There is an adjoining restaurant that serves lunch for about $20. It used to be a covered open-air cafeteria that served as a rainy-weather refuge. There is also a nearby snack bar with umbrellas over picnic tables, but the area is much smaller than the former cafeteria. There are also handy places to check extra baggage and clothing. After paying a modest fee at the Machu Picchu entrance booth, you are at your destination at last. It is now about 10:15 A.M. (10:15). If you will be taking the train back to Cusco that afternoon, check when you need to catch a bus back to Aguas Calientes, likely about 2:15 P.M. (14:15).

Using this guidebook and its maps, you can tour Machu Picchu in about four hours and visit all of the major sites and more. In addition, our descriptions, details and photos will enrich your experience all along the way. You will be able to fully enjoy this magnificent place between trains.

If you have time, however, try to stay overnight. There are many hotels and restaurants in Aguas Calientes to fit any budget, and buses depart for Machu Picchu as early as 6:30 A.M. (06:30). Be sure not to miss the last bus back down in the evening at about 5:00 P.M. (17:00), or you will be stranded and faced with a long, arduous hike down to Aguas Calientes. An extra day gives you the opportunity to take some of the Side Trips and to go back to your favorite places. If you get reservations for an overnight stay at the Sanctuary Lodge, you will have the special experience of sharing Machu Picchu with just a few other people after the last bus has left for Aguas Calientes, and hopefully you will be able to view a sunrise from the Guardhouse or up at Intipunku.

Weather

Cusco is at 11,000 feet (3,600 meters) elevation and Machu Picchu is at 8,040 (2,450 meters). Machu Picchu is 13 degrees below the equator, so their winter is our summer. However, the rainy season is from October through April, so the sunniest and warmest months are May through September. But there can be rain or sun any day of any month, as is typical in mountain environments. Often the mists swirl up from the Urubamba River early in the morning and then burn off by mid-morning. The wardrobe described below should work at any time of the year.

Clothing

Travel light. One carry-on bag and a backpack should be sufficient for a one- to two-week trip. Peruvians are casual, so women do not need skirts or dresses and men do not need a suit coat, but a tie may be useful. Take clothes that layer, for example slacks, long underwear or tights, short-sleeved and long-sleeved shirts, a sweater or vest, a warm fuzzy jacket, a windproof jacket that will also serve as rain gear (Gore-Tex® jacket and pants are ideal), a scarf and a hat. Take a travel umbrella. Shorts are not recommended for Machu Picchu (see "Bugs That Can Make You Itch"). Good footgear is critical as you will be on your feet all day. Take two pairs: one should be light hiking boots or good walking shoes (preferably waterproof) and the other, sneakers or running shoes. Of course, if you plan to hike the Inca Trail, take your regular mountaineering clothes.

Photography

Machu Picchu is a spectacular site for photography. We bring all of our film from our home country. Formerly we depended on our film shield bags to protect our film through the security machines at airports. However, with the explosive detection systems that have been installed at many U.S. and non-U.S. airports to scan (x-ray) checked baggage, stronger scanning equipment may jeopardize any unprocessed film that passes through the scanner. Kodak prepared a Technical Information Bulletin (TIB) on the subject. You can access it via the internet: www. kodak.com, then in the Search Box, type TIB5201 and click on the Search Button; then click on Index of TIBs; then click on Film Fog Issues (in Films Category); then click on TIB5201. You can now just read the material or print it out. Finally, a lightweight tripod is a must for telephoto shots and useful for other high quality photos.

Bugs That Can Make You Sick

Don't drink the water; don't use it for brushing teeth; don't eat fresh salads, and stay away from fresh fruit juices and unpasteurized milk. A little bit of caution will mean a healthy trip. Tea, coffee, beer, bottled drinks, and soups are good. You can buy bottled water. Most of the time we simply put tap water in a plastic bottle and add one pill of Potable Aqua or a similar product, and wait a half hour before drinking. The taste and color are a bit different, but it is safe. After the half hour, if you wish, you can add P.A. Plus Neutralizing Tablets, or equivalent, to get the water back to its original color and taste. These pills are available at outdoors and mountaineering stores. We have never become ill from drinking mixed drinks—Pisco Sours are a special favorite. All cooked foods are fine and pizza is popular.

Bugs That Can Make You Itch

There are tiny bugs that bite and can cause large, pink, itchy blotches. To prevent bites, use an insect repellent. Use a product like Cortaid if you are bitten. You will be wearing long pants, but protect your arms, neck, wrists and hands.

Money

We take cash and credit cards. Travel checks are harder to exchange. Use a money belt that fits around the waist (another reason for women to wear slacks) and that has room for your passport. Do not leave it in your hotel room. In Cusco most hotels and downtown restaurants accept credit cards. In more rural areas, or even in some restaurants off the main square in Cusco, you will need cash. Foreign money can be exchanged at airports, most hotels, or at the many small currency exchange shops along the streets in Cusco. The rates are quite similar. You can change extra Peruvian money back into your own currency at the Lima airport.

Miscellaneous

Take a lightweight flashlight; a small Spanish-English (or your language) dictionary and/or a phrase book; and a converter kit for electrical appliances such as hair dryers, shavers, and chargers, together with plugs appropriate for Peru (the kit tells you). In Cusco there are doctors, dentists, pharmacies, and shops where you can get most anything. It is a civilized country with friendly, helpful, and hardworking people.

Courtesy

A lot of damage done by tourists is due to thoughtlessness. The influx of tourists to archaeological sites, as well as to the natural wonders of our world, threatens the delicate balance of nature. Following a few simple rules can help preserve these wonderful places for future generations.

Obviously don't litter, don't pick the flowers and stay on designated trails to minimize erosion. There is still a lot of freedom of movement at Machu Picchu; however, there are a few rope barriers to protect some special places, such as the Intiwatana and the Ceremonial Rock. Do not climb over them! And the stone walls of Machu Picchu that may seem invulnerable are susceptible to damage from inadvertent scraping and chipping. Please respect the magnificent work and legacy of the Inca—and the Peruvians who are permitting us to share and enjoy their heritage.

Preface to the Revised Edition

Welcome to the revised edition. Since *The Machu Picchu Guidebook* was originally published, we have continued to visit the site, participating in ongoing explorations there, and we work to keep abreast of other research and new scholarship. There have been enough new developments that when our publisher asked us if we wanted to revise our book we jumped at the chance. There are four major additions that we think you will enjoy.

First: as a foldout at the end of the book, a beautiful and colorful artist's rendition of Machu Picchu as it appeared on the June 21 solstice celebration in the year 1530 at the height of the Inca Empire. Now when you look down at Machu Picchu from the Guardhouse area, it all comes to life with people, golden thatched roofs, farm workers, llamas going through the main gate with their packs, and preparations for the festival. The art first appeared in the May 2002 map supplement of *National Geographic* magazine, and the magazine and artist Robert Guisti generously gave us permission to publish it here. Ken and coauthors Ruth Wright and Alfredo Valencia Zegarra were consultants to *National Geographic*, and one of our photographs was used as the basis for the painting. We have also added an additional eight-page section of color illustrations where we selected details from the artist's rendition of the site as it might have looked five hundred years ago and paired them with photographs of the same location as they appear today.

Second: We produced a whole new substitute chapter on the extraordinary structures near the top of Huayna Picchu Mountain. New investigations, surveys, sketches, measurements, photographs, and archaeological interpretations show a rich array and intense use of Huayna Picchu by the Inca. Never again need visitors simply climb Huayna Picchu for the view, but they also will be able to experience it as a holy mountain complementing Machu Picchu as a sacred center. A map showing all of its details leads the reader through its intricacies.

Third: It was long suspected that the wide staircase leading from the check station halfway up the Inca Trail to Intipunko (Gate of the Sun) and abruptly cut off by the dense forest would lead to additional discoveries. As soon as we started clearing the forest in 2002, four stone steps appeared that took us onto a platform that would have had both ceremonial and security functions. After more determined clearing, a well built trail was uncovered that eventually led to the ridge of Machu Picchu and then beyond. The trail remains impassable.

Fourth: a new book, *Field Guide to the Birds of Machu Picchu, Peru*, inspired us to present a short chapter on this important wildlife aspect of the Machu Picchu Sanctuary. Over 400 species are recorded in the book with fine colored paintings, including the Inca Wren, found nowhere else in the world. Where and how to purchase the field guide is described.

We also spent time examining unfinished construction and concluded that Machu Picchu was still a work in process with additional temples, walls, and terraces to be completed. In any case, we hope that the guidebook will add to your enjoyment of this magnificent place and help you to appreciate the rich legacy of the Inca.

RMW

Preface to the First Edition

This guide will provide you with insights into the wonders and details of the royal estate and religious center of the Inca emperor Pachacuti. Whether you have three hours or three days at Machu Picchu, we want to help you see things of significance that otherwise might blend in with the overall grand impressions of this "Lost City of the Inca." For accuracy of interpretation, the book taps into the work of respected explorers, archaeologists, scientists, architects, engineers, and others, from Hiram Bingham's discoveries to the latest explorations on the east flank of Machu Picchu.

My coauthor, Dr. Alfredo Valencia Zegarra, has devoted his entire professional life to the study and research of the ancient Andean civilizations. His first job was as resident archaeologist at Machu Picchu, and as a result he knows every nook and cranny. He excavated and reconstructed the Sacred Rock area and is the reigning expert on the Temple of the Condor. In 1992 he and his wife, Arminda Gibaja Oviedo, published a book that summarizes and analyzes all the excavations done at Machu Picchu since Hiram Bingham was there. Dr. Valencia's knowledge, thoughts, and opinions on Machu Picchu are invaluable contributions to this book.

As for me, I first visited Machu Picchu in 1974 with an archaeological group. Besides being awed by the magnificent setting and stonework, I wondered where the Inca got their water on this ridge-top site. Then, in 1994, an archaeological permit from the Instituto Nacional de Cultura de Peru was issued to answer that question. It soon became an objective of the research team, however, to study much more: How was the community planned? How did it function? The more we learned, the more we marveled at the competence of the engineers and builders who were able to construct a functioning masterpiece on this spectacular but difficult site. We found that the miracle of Machu Picchu is in its details.

We hope, by leading you through Machu Picchu with our maps, photographs, and the details and insights we have gleaned from many fine sources and innumerable days on-site, that you can share what we have learned. The Inca are well worth knowing, and perhaps this guide will help bring them, and Machu Picchu, to life.

RMW

ELNOVENOINGA
PACHACVTIINGA
IVPANQVI

Reynoyas   ta chile y se to   dasucordelliea
                                              pachaquti

Inca Pachacuti in war regalia with his mace and shield.

DEPOCITODELINGA
COLLCA

topaynga
yupanqui

[...] rushador
suyo yoc
apo pomachava

depocitos del ynga

como

A quipu keeper reporting the contents of the qolqas (collca) to a nobleman. The keeper recorded information by use of knots on strings.

Introduction

In one of the most spectacular settings on earth, the great Inca ruler Pachacuti built a royal retreat and sacred center that is known as Machu Picchu. Commenced in the middle of the fifteenth century, it was used by Pachacuti and his *panaca* (royal corporate family group), who continued to improve the site until the empire was destroyed by the conquering Spaniards in the 1530s. Though there is evidence that the Spaniards were aware of a place called Piccho, there is no record that they ever visited this site. Certainly, the sacred rocks, defaced by Spaniards in other locations, remained intact here. Centuries of jungle growth enveloped the great granite structures and temples, like the castle in "Sleeping Beauty," for more than three hundred fifty years. Then, in 1911, a young American explorer named Hiram Bingham (Fig. 1) led an expedition into the Urubamba Valley, looking for a "lost city of the Incas." Fortunately (with help from local Indians) he found Machu Picchu and spent the next few years reclaiming and rescuing it from the jungle. His articles and photographs for *National Geographic* magazine stunned the world. Since then archaeologists and engineers, writers and photographers, and thousands of visitors have been enthralled and inspired by this mystical place.

Machu Picchu is built on a narrow ridge between Machu Picchu Mountain and Huayna Picchu Mountain at an elevation of 8,040 feet (2,450 meters), 13 degrees south of the Equator (Fig. 2). The ridge drops off steeply on both sides to the Urubamba River 1,500 feet (450 meters) below. The river circles the site on three sides and eventually joins the Amazon. Because of its lower elevation and proximity to the rain forest, Machu Picchu has a wetter and milder climate than Cusco.

In Inca times you would have traveled for more than a week on the Inca Trail to get from the Inca capital at Cusco to Machu

Figure 1. Explorer Hiram Bingham on location at Machu Picchu in 1912

Figure 2. View of Machu Picchu from Huayna Picchu

Picchu, stopping at *tambos* (way stations) along the route. Eventually you would have reached Intipunku (Gate of the Sun) and the final descent to Machu Picchu. What an awesome sight to behold: beautiful agricultural terraces, the city beyond with grand plazas, hundreds of thatched-roof stone buildings, temples, and a striking peak, Huayna Picchu, as backdrop. Forested mountain ranges and snowcapped peaks set if off like a jewel. There may have been mists swirling up from the Urubamba River Valley, creating an aura of mystery (Fig. 3). If you were fortunate, you would be invited into the city.

There are many different ways to experience Machu Picchu. We hope this guidebook will give you the tools to do it in your own way. In the last several decades, much has been learned about the Inca in general and Machu Picchu in particular. Since the Inca had no written language, scientists have had to "read" their artifacts, their stones, their temples, and their mummies to

Figure 3. Machu Picchu with mist rising from the Urubamba River

establish their place in history. Recent information and new analyses of earlier findings are shedding additional light on these truly remarkable people and their culture.

The arrangement of this guide is such that you can choose your own route through Machu Picchu. The text and the fold-out map (at back of book) are coordinated. The map has red lines, which we call Tourist Routes, that lead you through the site. The city is architecturally (and conveniently) divided into *conjuntos* (groups of buildings often surrounded by a wall). We have numbered them 1 through 18 on the map, and the buildings and rooms within the conjuntos are also numbered. The peripheral areas are lettered A though F. While Machu Picchu is actually built on a southeast-northwest axis, for simplification of orientation, consider Huayna Picchu Mountain to be north.

Looking at the map, you can see that the city is laid out very differently from the cities of medieval Europe. In Europe there

Figure 4. Thatched-roof Guardhouse, a good place to start your tour

is usually a central plaza, with a church or cathedral and many narrow streets radiating out from it in a somewhat haphazard but charming fashion. Machu Picchu is highly structured. There is an Agricultural Sector separated from the Urban Sector by the City Wall. The Agricultural Sector is divided into Upper and Lower Agricultural Sectors by the main Inca Trail from Cusco. The Urban Sector is separated into Western and Eastern Sectors by wide green plazas.

Although you can choose your own route, we will start at the thatched-roof Guardhouse up on the ridge (Fig. 4). (The names, such as "Guardhouse," that have been assigned to buildings and areas by Bingham and others, though based on conjecture, are generally appropriate.) At this location you will get a breathtaking view of the Machu Picchu site and will see it as the ancients saw it coming down the Inca Trail. You will get a holistic view of Machu Picchu, rather than piecing it together from its fascinating but individual parts.

If you decide to not take this route, enter through the usual tourist entrance between the storehouses (Area E). Then, using the foldout map and chapter headings, you can find the information on each area as you visit it.

The Guardhouse
and the Terrace of the
Ceremonial Rock

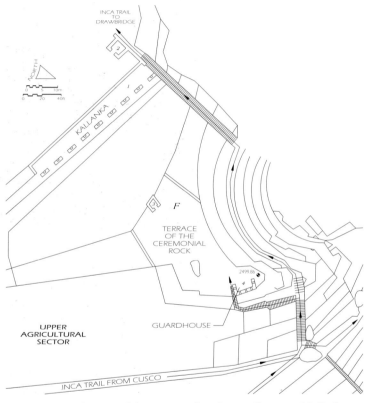

Figure 5. Map of Terrace of the Ceremonial Rock, Guardhouse, and *kallanka*

Figure 6. Inca domestic water supply canal and storehouse

You can reach the Guardhouse (in eight to ten minutes) by taking the trail and steps to the left (marked "Trail to Guardhouse" on the foldout map) shortly after passing through the ticket entrance from the hotel area. As you go up the stairs you will see five two-storied buildings on your right. These were food storehouses and living areas for agricultural workers.

After five short switchbacks, you will be on a narrow terrace just above the uppermost storehouse, where a small stone-lined canal emerges from the forested area on the left heading toward the royal estate (Fig. 6). This is the Inca domestic water supply canal that carried pure water from a spring on the north face of Machu Picchu Mountain to the sixteen fountains in the heart of the enclave. (See "Inca Water Management.") Eight more switchbacks take you to the Inca Trail from Cusco and a large, flat rock platform for your first great view of Machu Picchu. From here you can proceed up the Inca Trail or down to the Main Gate; instead, go up the nearby stairs to the Guardhouse and the Terrace of the Ceremonial Rock.

From here you can see the overall grand design of Machu Picchu: the elegant agricultural terraces emphasizing the natural contours of the hillsides, the Urban Sector divided by a giant green swath into Western and Eastern Sectors, and the inspired man-made structures using and enhancing this spectacular and challenging ridge-top site. Huayna Picchu Mountain is a stunning backdrop, as are the surrounding mountains (Fig. 7). The Urubamba River, unseen from here in its deep canyon, winds around three sides. To visualize what Machu Picchu looked like from here in Inca times, turn to the artist's rendition created for the *National Geographic* magazine in May 2002. It is located on the back of the foldout map of Machu Picchu at the back of the book. It depicts Machu Picchu as it appeared at the height of the Inca Empire in 1530 A.D. on June 21 during a celebration of the Winter Solstice. The granite stones have not yet weathered to gray, the roofs are a fresh yellow thatch, and llamas are entering the Main Gate to deposit their packs in the storehouse. Note that the storehouse has been opened up (cutaway) to reveal the likely structure of the roof supports. There is also a color photo section of "after and before" pictures showing the comparison between scenes at Machu Picchu today and how the artist has brought them to life. If you have the time, after you have toured the royal retreat, you may want to come back up to this location again and find your favorite places on the painting.

The Guardhouse is in the *wayrona* style, that is, three-sided and open on one of its long sides. The Guardhouse opens up to the Terrace of the Ceremonial Rock with its large, beautifully carved and polished rock (Fig. 8). The rock was brought to the site for ceremonial purposes. The symbolism of the slanted surface, the steps, and the ring carefully cut on one side is unknown, but we can admire the craftsmanship required in its creation, using only hammerstones, bronze tools, and sand. It is surrounded by round river rocks, symbolically bringing the powerful and sacred river to this mountain site (Fig. 9). The river rocks are now scattered and insignificant looking, but were

Figure 7. View of Machu Picchu with Uña Picchu and Huayna Picchu in background

Figure 8. Ceremonial Rock (foreground), Guardhouse, and Huayna Picchu (background)

Figure 9. Ritually significant river rocks surrounding Ceremonial Rock

ritually important at one time. Formerly, walls on either side also set this area apart. The function of the small building, No. 3 in Figure 5, is unknown.

Beyond the ceremonial rock and on a higher terrace sits the largest building at Machu Picchu. It was a *kallanka*, or great hall, with many entrances. A *kallanka* was usually built on the main plaza of an Inca city, where festivities and ceremonies were held for the common folk, and was particularly useful in bad weather. As a royal estate, however, the city beyond the wall was reserved for the Inca elite, their retinue, and the permanent residents. Instead, the farmers and other workers from the surrounding area could be invited to this splendid site for festivities on the outskirts of the royal retreat. The many potsherds (pieces of broken pottery) found in the area, mostly drinking vessels, confirm that drinking *chicha*, the ceremonial maize (corn) beer, was an essential activity at these events. Different levels of terraces could be accessed by using the so-called flying steps cantilevered from the terrace walls (Fig.10).

Figure 10. Flying steps provided access to *kallanka* entrance

From this location your eye can follow the Inca Trail up to Intipunku (Gate of the Sun) where a few structures indicate that it was an important final checkpoint for travelers descending to the royal estate. (See "Side Trip: Intipunku [Gate of the Sun].") Several terraces downhill from the Guardhouse, another trail leads to the Inca Drawbridge and formerly continued on the west side of Machu Picchu Mountain. (See "Side Trip: Inca Drawbridge.")

Now head to the Main Gate. More than 100 well-constructed agricultural terraces come into view. In fact Machu Picchu owes its longevity to the terraces. The site map and aerial photo (Figs. 11 and 12) show that there are two major geologic faults, the

Figure 11. Site map of Machu Picchu and environs, including the Machu Picchu and Huayna Picchu Faults

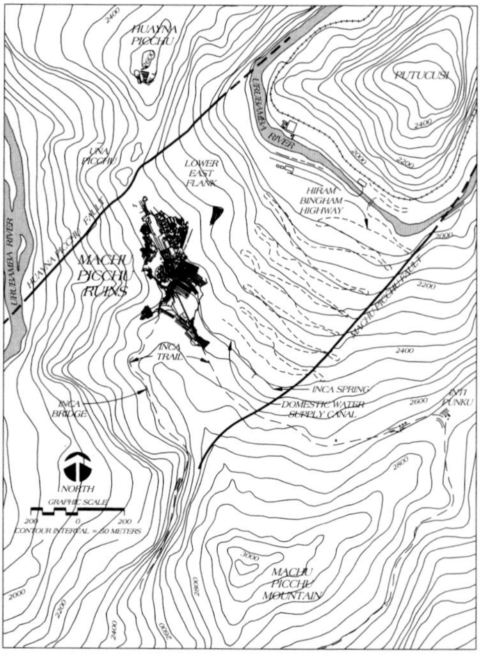

Figure 12. Aerial photo of Machu Picchu and environs

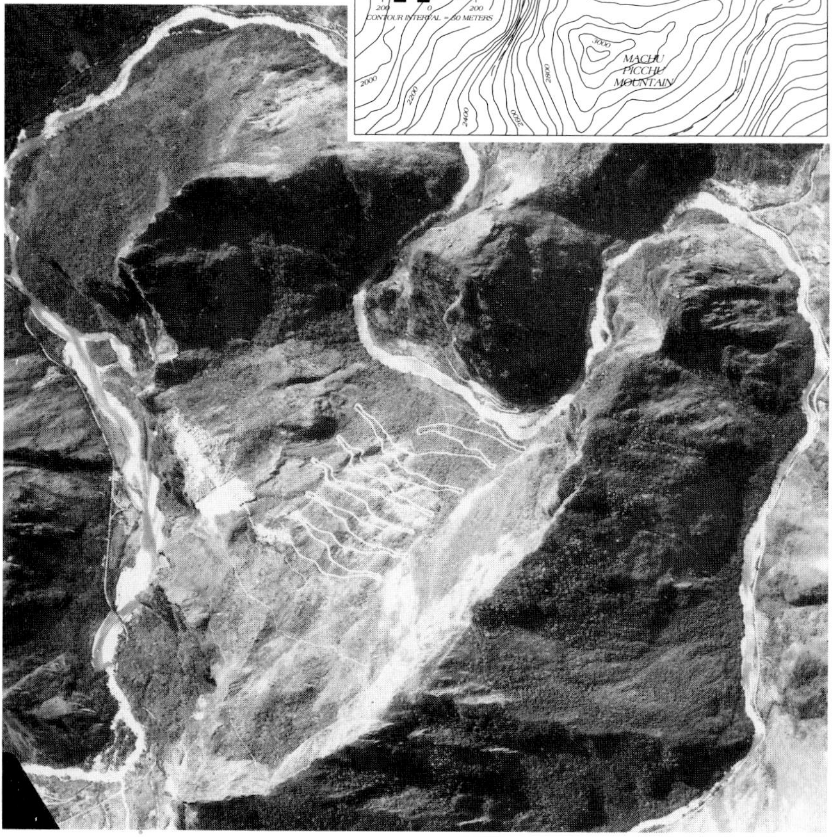

Machu Picchu Fault and the Huayna Picchu Fault. These high-angle reverse faults formed a wedge-shaped structural block that dropped relative to the peaks on either side. This block, or graben, is the ridge on which the Inca built their retreat, with Machu Picchu Mountain and Huayna Picchu Mountain on either side. Enormous effort was put into this virtually unbuildable site by constructing hundreds of walls to create flat spaces. Some 60 percent of the construction at Machu Picchu lies underground, providing foundations and drainage for the buildings and walls — an impressive engineering feat. But the Machu Picchu Fault also permitted the development of a perennial spring, without which the site would probably not have been chosen. (See "Inca Water Management.") In addition, the jumble of rocks from the faulting meant that there was a ready supply of granite building materials.

Figure 13. Dry Moat, a drainage channel dividing the agricultural and urban areas, with survey rock in foreground

Just before you reach the Main Gate, there is a wide ditch heading straight downhill, called the Dry Moat. It provides another separation between the agricultural and urban areas and is also a drainage channel. A major staircase runs all the way down to the main pathway. Eventually you may want to go down this staircase, or up it from below, because it provides the best view of the Lower Agricultural Sector, the domestic water supply canal where it crosses the Dry Moat and goes underneath the City Wall, and the second water supply canal that was in progress when the city was abandoned. (See "Various Sights on the Way Out.") A rather sharp rock juts up along the staircase about one-third of the way down. It likely functioned as a survey marker (Fig. 13).

The clouds part to reveal mystical Machu Picchu.

View from Uña Picchu in late afternoon with the Intiwatana pyramid on the right, the Eastern Urban Sector in full sunlight, and the agricultural terraces beyond.

The Western Sector with the round
wall of the Temple of the Sun,
separated from the Eastern Urban
Sector by the wide green plazas.

One of the windows of the Temple of the
Three Windows frames the Artisans' Wall;
llamas graze in the plaza.

The Temple of the Three Windows is a
focal point of the view through a
window of the Eastern Urban Sector.

A panorama of the Eastern Urban Sector with the Temple of the Condor in the lower right.

A long granite staircase leads down to the Artisans' Wall; Yanantin Mountain peeks over the clouds, and the rounded Putucusi looms in the center, both on the other side of the Urubamba River.

The circular Temple of the Sun, the thatched-roofed *wayrona*, and the Royal Residence are a suitable terminal for the one-half-mile-long water canal on the left.

The morning sun highlights the natural Intiwatana pyramid, which lies north of the Sacred Plaza, with the Principal Temple in the lower center and the Temple of the Three Windows on the right.

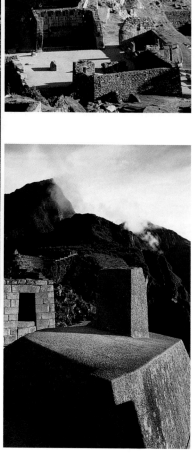

The long granite staircase seen here from inside an Eastern Urban Sector building; a llama surveys the scene.

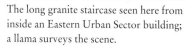

The beautifully sculpted Intiwatana stone with late afternoon shadows; it is not a sun dial nor a solar observatory.

A storm has passed, creating a dramatic contrast between the sun-bathed Eastern Urban Sector and the mountains beyond.

The triangular *in situ* rock is carved in the shape of a condor with a ruff; the natural rocks behind it form huge outspread wings, hence the name Temple of the Condor.

Machu Picchu is a mecca for photographers — many say a bad picture cannot be taken there.

Sharing the same view the Inca nobility had from inside the *wayrona* adjacent to the Temple of the Sun: sacred Putucusi Mountain on the right and the mountains of the Urubamba Valley receding into the distance.

The curved terraces of the Upper Agricultural Sector are dominated by the Guardhouse on the left and the *kallanka* with sunlit doorways to the right.

Looking down on the Guardhouse with a telescopic lens from the summit of Huayna Picchu; the Inca trail angles to the left.

Even the buildings of Machu Picchu were designed to be in geometric harmony with the mountain backdrop.

A llama at rest in the Main Plaza in a tranquil scene dominated by Machu Picchu Mountain.

The exquisite sculpted stone at the entrance of the Royal Tomb with high niches inside demonstrates the importance of the cave beneath the Temple of the Sun.

The Western Urban Sector

The urban area of Machu Picchu is divided into Western and Eastern Sectors. The Western Sector is considered the *hanan* or upper area, both geographically and socially.

The Main Gate and Conjunto 1

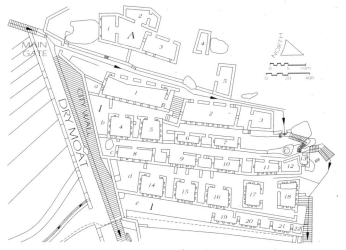

Figure 14. Map of Conjunto 1

Descending stairs lead to the impressive Main Gate with its huge lintel, or stone beam across the doorway. The wall that juts out on the left would have made the gate easier to control, if such was necessary. Although not a military outpost in the usual sense, Machu Picchu is located near the eastern reaches of the empire and was reasonably defensible, with steep slopes on three sides

Figure 15. View of Huayna Picchu through the Main Gate

Figure 16. Bingham team's sketch showing how the Main Gate may have operated

and a narrow ridge approach on the fourth. In addition, the timbers of the Inca Drawbridge could be completely removed, preventing access from that quarter. There was also an outer wall, shown on the map just to the left of the trail to the Guardhouse, parts of which can be seen near the tourist entrance and elsewhere.

The Main Gate frames a view of Huayna Picchu (Fig. 15). It is obvious from this and other sites that the Inca set a premium on views of mountains and other natural features. Time and again we are impressed by the effort and thought that went into framing and incorporating the natural beauty of the place and its surroundings. The natural features not only satisfied their aesthetic sense but also held great religious significance and fit into the Inca worldview. A stone ring protrudes just above the door on the inside of the gate, and barholds are recessed into the doorjambs on both sides a few feet above the floor. Bingham's team made a sketch of the likely closure mechanism using these features (Fig. 16).

This is the front door. The Inca ruler and his family, priests and other dignitaries, and their retinue would have entered here with

Figure 17. The Inca ruler and his queen traveled comfortably

17

great pomp, some having been carried by porters along the Inca Trail from Cusco (Fig. 17). However, it was also the front door for deliveries. The wide area just inside the entrance would have been used by llama pack trains delivering goods. The packs could easily be transferred to the storehouses that line the path on the right side. Room 1 was two stories high—you can still see the ledge that supported a wooden second floor. This is the building that is pictured as a "cut-away" in the artist's rendition of Machu Picchu. On the left side are two narrow cuts in the wall with a few steps up to a terrace—a handy temporary corral for the agile llamas.

You are now in Conjunto 1. We use the word *conjunto* to represent a group of buildings, usually but not necessarily surrounded by a wall, that are part of a single complex. Machu Picchu was planned as a series of separate conjuntos (which we have

Figure 18. Double-jamb doorway, used for entrances to special places

numbered 1 through 18) with paths or stairways leading from one to the other. These 18 conjuntos are illustrated on the fold-out map. (Note the small blue arrows that indicate drain holes that were incorporated into the walls at the time of construction.) Conjunto 1 has five different levels with storehouses, residences, and what were probably workshops.

Continue down the ramp and proceed to a sharp right turn, where you will encounter your first double-jamb doorway. Only the lower part remains (Fig. 18). A double-jamb doorway was an architectural feature used for entrances to special places, the double jamb usually being on the outside, as you will see later. This doorway is unique in Machu Picchu, seemingly backward because it appears to signify a special exit—the final ramp leading up to the Main Gate. The steps then lead past a small room (No. 13 on the map), possibly for stationing a sentry. As you temporarily exit Conjunto 1, uphill on the left you will see the extensive granite Rock Quarry, a source of the building material used throughout Machu Picchu. Ahead is the Sacred Plaza and beyond lies the Intiwatana. But your next route is partway down the longest staircase in Machu Picchu, the Stairway of the Fountains. Go down the stairway and enter the lowest level of Conjunto 1 at Rooms 19 to 22. From these rooms you can look down for an overview of Conjunto 2.

The Temple of the Sun, the Royal Mausoleum and Conjunto 2

(*Note:* If you have been taking your own route and are coming up the stairs from below Conjunto 2, go first to the lowest terrace of Conjunto 1 to look down onto Conjunto 2.)

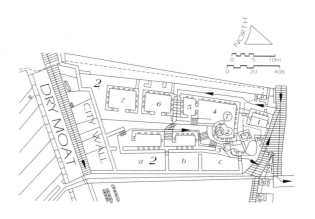

Figure 19. Map of Conjunto 2

From your vantage point on the lowest terrace of Conjunto 1 (Rooms 19 to 22, or even farther along the terrace), look straight down to the main Inca water supply canal on its own special terrace. The stone-lined canal is typically about 5 inches wide and 4 inches deep. Springwater from the flanks of Machu Picchu Mountain was brought in this canal via gravity flow to a series of sixteen fountains to be used for domestic and ceremonial purposes. To the right you can see where the canal passes under the City Wall. From there it goes to Fountain 1, on the left, the first and highest fountain, with the purest water.

From here you also have the best view of one of the most holy and private conjuntos in Machu Picchu (Fig. 20). Here is the great structure called the Temple of the Sun, probably because its fine curved wall is reminiscent of the Coricancha (Temple of the Sun) in Cusco. It is also called the Torreon (tower). Bingham simply called it the Semicircular Temple. The Temple is con-

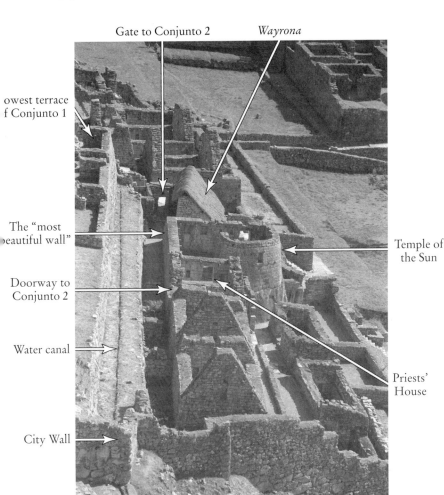

Gate to Conjunto 2   *Wayrona*

owest terrace
f Conjunto 1

The "most
beautiful wall"

Doorway to
Conjunto 2

Water canal

City Wall

Temple of
the Sun

Priests'
House

Figure 20. Conjunto 2, one of the holiest conjuntos in Machu Picchu

structed on a natural rock formation and partially encircles the top of that specially cut rock formation with the finest stonework of Machu Picchu (Fig. 21). The sacred rock that takes up most of the space inside the curved wall was honored and protected by the Inca masonry that surrounded it. It was recently learned that the straight ledge, which was created by cutting away part of the rock (Fig. 22), bisects the sunlight passing through the eastern window at sunrise on June 21, the winter solstice. Therefore, the Temple of the Sun can be considered a

Figure 21. Temple of the Sun, which served as a solar observatory, with Priests' House on the right

Figure 22. The sacred rock within the Temple of the Sun showing the ledge cutaway

Figure 23. Bingham called this "the most beautiful wall in America"

Figure 24. Fountain 1, which served, like all the fountains here, as a domestic water supply

Figure 25. Double-jamb doorway into Conjunto 2 has traditional trapezoidal shape

23

solar observatory. The rock and some of the wall stones are cracked, perhaps due to a fire sometime in its past. From here you can also see that a platform joins the Priests' House (on the right). One can imagine priests coming out of the door in full ceremonial vestments for religious ceremonies at the Temple. To the left of the Temple is a thatched-roof building. It is a *wayrona*, like the Guardhouse, and is an integral part of this complex, as are Fountains 1, 2 and 3. The western wall of the Temple of the Sun is a long, straight wall that Bingham called "the most beautiful wall in America" (Fig. 23).

Leave Conjunto 1 the way you came, take the stairway down to the next level, and go through the entrance to Fountain 1 immediately on the right (Fig. 24). Though the fountains all have the same basic design—a small channel to concentrate the jet of water, a shallow rectangular basin below, sidewalls with niches, an outlet for water to flow to the next fountain, and an entrance for people to fill their *aryballos* (pottery bottles), each fountain has its own character. The many potsherds found in and around the fountains attest to their use as a domestic water supply. A special feature of Fountain 1 is a curved channel cut into the rock to take the water under the path over to Fountain 2, located between the *wayrona* and the "most beautiful wall." It is indeed a fine wall of coursed, matched stones, which leads to a complete and particularly beautiful double-jamb doorway (Fig. 25). Here the double jamb is on the outside, the usual location, announcing the special place beyond. Built in the traditional trapezoidal shape of Inca doorways, windows, and niches, it is topped by a great lintel. On the inside, a large stone ring protrudes above the door and barholds are located on each side, similar to the Main Gate, indicating that it also had some sort of door or closure (Fig. 26). Figure 27 shows that these structures were intact when Bingham found them.

A stairway cut into one huge block of stone (another technique used by the ingenious Inca stonemasons) takes you down to the next level. Then, on the left, is the lower level of the Priests' House (Building 5 in Fig. 19), where you can still see the inside ledge that held up the former wooden floor of the second floor. Inside stairways were a rarity in Inca buildings, so the outside

Ring

Barhold

Figure 26. Double-jamb doorway viewed from inside showing barholds and ring

Figure 27. Same double-jamb doorway, photographed by Bingham

stairway leading up to the Temple of the Sun would also have been used to access the second floor. The photograph of the inside of "the most beautiful wall" shows that it is lined with a row of niches and pegs (Fig. 28).

The magnificent curved wall of the Temple of the Sun looms ahead. Note the south window with its four stone protuberances, which were likely used for astronomical/observatory purposes. The stonemasons integrated the Temple into the natural rock

Figure 28. Inside of "the most beautiful wall" showing pegs and niches

Figure 29. Temple of the Sun, viewed from the south

formation to create one remarkable unified whole (Fig. 29). Note that the wall leans slightly inward for stability and that the stone layers decrease in height progressively from bottom to top, both being practical and aesthetically pleasing. Carved into the rock base is just the hint of five steps—intriguing and inexplicable. From this side you can see why it is called a "torreon" (tower).

Figure 30. Natural cave below Temple of the Sun, which Bingham called the Royal Mausoleum or Tomb

Figure 31. Sculpted stone inside the cave

Figure 32. High niches inside the cave

Figure 33. Hourglass-shaped stonework at the entrance of the cave exemplifies the genius of Inca artisans

Figure 34. View from inside the cave

Figure 35. Fountains 5 and 6 in the Stairway of the Fountains

Figure 36. Map of the Temple of the Sun, fountains, and Royal Residence

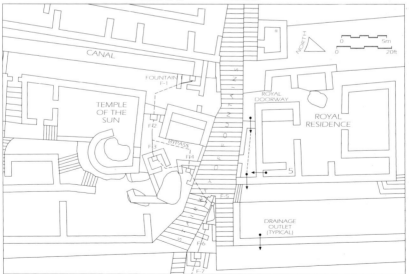

Figure 37. Enigmatic Window on the north side of the Temple of the Sun, framing the Guardhouse

Beneath the Temple of the Sun is a natural cave, part of the same rock formation, which Bingham called the Royal Mausoleum or Tomb (Fig. 30). (See "Mummies.") Although no remains were found here, it was a place of special significance. Note the exquisitely carved, stepped white stone at the entrance; the low carved stone on the floor (Fig. 31) with a shape similar to the Intiwatana stone, which you will see later; the unusually high niches (Fig. 32); and the stones between the stepped stone and the natural rock on the right, carefully fitted into an hourglass shape (Fig. 33). This stonework and the integration of the components exemplify the genius of Inca artisans to meld natural and man-made features into an aesthetic whole. There is even a stunning shadow play from inside the cave (Fig. 34); however, visitors are not allowed inside.

From the Royal Mausoleum go north through a breach in the wall to the Stairway of the Fountains. (See a diagram of the 16 fountains in Fig. 129, page 109.) Note that this breach in the Inca

Figure 38. Carved and polished sacred rock at Fountain 3, the Sacred Fountain

wall violates the spirit and design of this exceptionally private, religious area. The wall was intact in Bingham's 1915 map and sketch and was opened later, probably as a convenience for tourists.

Once you are through the breach, go down several steps. The Staircase of the Fountains is divided here, making way for Fountains 5 and 6, an inspired combination (Fig. 35). (Water would continue to flow from one fountain to the next until Fountain 16, which serviced the Temple of the Condor.) At some time during your visit you may want to go all the way down the Stairway of the Fountains to appreciate the diversity of design and the sound of falling water, just as the Inca heard it. From this location, look to the north side of the stairway to see a special drainage channel that carried rainwater from the front door of the Royal Residence (to the right of the stairway in Fig. 36). This channel also intercepted the flushed bathing water from Room 5 of the Royal Residence.

Now go up the steps to the *wayrona* (Building 1 in Fig. 19, page 20), which has one side open to a spectacular view of the valley and the mountains and to ceremonies that would have been performed here. Chalk lines on the walls inside the *wayrona* and other buildings are used by archaeologists to track movement and building settlement. You saw the geologic fault lines illustrated in Figure 11 (page 12): Machu Picchu is in an earthquake zone. Water seeping beneath the structures also adds to the instability.

The Temple of the Sun has a unique window on this north side. Its function is unclear and, therefore, it has been named the Enigmatic Window (Fig. 37). There are several holes bored all the way through the stones that are reminiscent of holes in the doorways and windows of the Coricancha in Cusco, which Spanish chroniclers reported were decorated with glittering gold and silver artifacts. Perhaps the holes were used to fasten objects to the window.

Here also is Fountain 3, the Sacred Fountain, with its own carved and smoothly polished ceremonial rock (Fig. 38). Water played a very significant role in Inca life and religion. Sources of water were revered, and some springs were even believed to be entrances to mountains used by mountain gods. Four essential elements came together here—mountains, rocks, sun, and water—to make this a highly significant and spiritual site.

Running along the base of the *wayrona* is a bypass channel that takes water from just above Fountain 3 and discharges it directly into Fountain 4 (Fig. 36). At present, water that flows into Fountain 3 never reaches Fountain 4 because settlement of the rock formations has opened up routes for water to flow down into cracks and fissures, contributing to the instability of the site. Some building stones are leaning away from their original positions, and there is considerable water staining inside the Royal Tomb underneath. It is likely that the bypass channel did not exist in Inca times. It does not appear in Bingham's sketches of Machu Picchu, and our research demonstrates that his sketches usually portrayed such details accurately.

The Royal Residence (Conjunto 3)

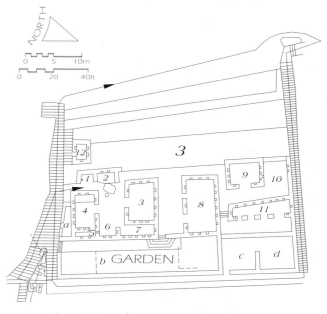

Figure 39. Map of Conjunto 3, the Royal Residence

A few steps up and to the right is the entrance to the Royal Residence. Although it may have been used by an elite Inca such as a high priest, it is generally assumed that Inca Pachacuti and his family resided here when they visited their royal estate. It is really designed to house just one elite family, with support from staff to satisfy their every need. A small building (No. 12 in Fig. 39), just above the entrance and facing the stairway, probably served as a sentry station. Notice that the walls leading to the entrance of the Royal Residence are made of stones cut with a puffy, or pillow-like look, which sets off each stone as an individual—a different technique again (Fig. 40). Somewhat surprisingly, the entrance to the residence is not a double-jamb door,

Figure 40. Entrance to the Royal Residence lined with rocks cut in pillow-like shapes

Figure 41. Large horizontal stone ring just inside Royal Residence may have been used to hold a torch or staff

nor does it have a closure mechanism. Just inside, in what we might call a foyer (No. 1), there is a large horizontal stone ring protruding from the wall about six feet off the floor. This ring was carved from a huge rock that starts on the other side of the wall, showing the innovative use of a natural feature. It may have been a receptacle for a torch or staff (Fig. 41).

The Inca ruler visiting his royal retreat would have been well taken care of here. It is very private, with easy access to the religious ceremonies at the Temple of the Sun, the Sacred Plaza, the Intiwatana, and, not incidentally, the purest water at Fountain 1.

There was a central open (not roofed) courtyard with two large rooms across from each other and *wayrona*-like structures on either end. The large room on the south side (No. 4) is thought to be the bedroom of the Inca. The entrance is huge, spanned by a single lintel of truly majestic proportions (Fig. 42). The purpose of the thin line incised across the lintel and inside the bedroom at about the same level is unknown. The huge lintel above the

Figure 42. Doorway to what is probably the bedroom is spanned by a huge lintel with an etched line

doorway on the other side of the courtyard has cracked, possibly because it is not as thick. (As you go through other doorways at Machu Picchu, look up to note that there are usually two lintels side by side sharing the weight of the wall above.)

The Inca did not have our kind of furniture. They incorporated niches and pegs into the walls for storage. They built raised platforms on the floors and perhaps placed alpaca skins and blankets on top to make beds or places to sit. One can imagine layers of blankets for sleeping comfort. Their houses were plastered on the inside with either gypsum or fine clay in light colors. (There is a house in Ollantaytambo that has been completely restored, and the interior is bright and pleasant.) Given their love of, and talent for, making fine textiles, it is also reasonable to suppose that they had wall hangings. Figure 43 is an illustration of an Inca queen with a mirror in one hand being groomed by handmaidens and a dwarf hunchback holding a bowl of water for her hands. They are wearing the traditional capes held together

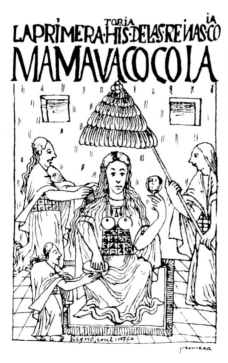

Figure 43. Inca queen being groomed by attendants, with a hunchbacked dwarf holding a bowl of water for cleansing her hands

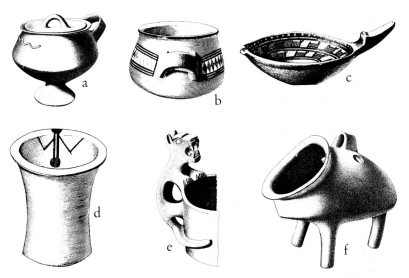

Figure 44. Household and ceremonial pottery found at Machu Picchu: (a) cooking pot; (b) two-handled dish; (c) drinking ladle with bird's-head handle; (d) *kero*, or cup; (e) handle in form of jaguar; (f) brazier.

by stick pins or *tupus*. The queen has two large *tupus* attached to her cape. She appears to be seated, perhaps on cloths, and there is a "rug" on the floor. Various household and ceremonial items found at Machu Picchu are shown in Figure 44.

Room 5 was likely a "bathroom" with its own drainage system through the wall and connecting to the drainage channel you saw on the north side of the Stairway of the Fountains. Blackened sherds were found in Room 7, indicating that it was the cooking area. There was a private garden ("b" in Fig. 39, page 35) and a corral ("c" and "d"), where meat on the hoof, probably llamas, would have been kept.

The Rock Quarry

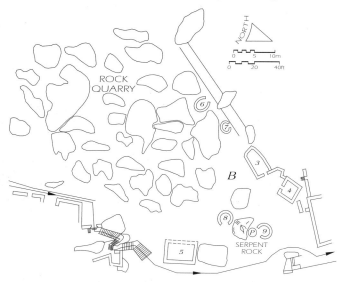

Figure 45. Map of the Quarry (Peripheral Area B)

Continue up the Stairway of the Fountains to the Quarry. The broken granite here and elsewhere was the result of the geologic faults and seismic forces. The availability of such excellent granite must also have been a factor in choosing this site. You will see the small circular foundations that were likely huts used by the stoneworkers (Nos. 6, 7, 8 and 9 in Fig. 45). Figure 46 shows features of the site. The "Serpent Rock" has several snakes etched onto its surface, which were featured in Bingham's early descriptions (Fig. 47). These are rather crudely done and can be seen only by climbing onto the rock. ("P" in Fig. 45 denotes petroglyph.) Do not be fooled by the rock a modern archaeologist used to experiment with splitting techniques. He used the method of the ancient Egyptians—not the Inca! (Fig. 48). The Inca workmen used hammerstones, hundreds of which were found in this area by Hiram Bingham and others. Some are still around today. They

Split   Hut   Serpent
rock   foundation   Rock

Figure 46. Quarry with split rock, hut foundation, and Serpent Rock

Figure 47. Serpent Rock, etched with several snake designs

Figure 48. Rock split by modern archaeologist using ancient Egyptian technique

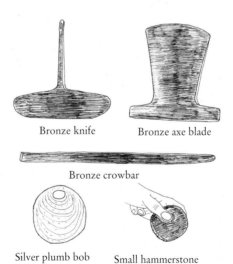

Bronze knife   Bronze axe blade

Bronze crowbar

Silver plumb bob   Small hammerstone

Figure 49. Hammerstone and bronze and silver tools used by Inca workmen

also used bronze and silver tools (Fig. 49) and were able to take advantage of the natural fractures in the rocks (Fig. 50). There is also a large rock that is cut to create steps similar to the rock steps seen in the Temple of the Sun.

You may wonder what happened to the innumerable chips that were hammered off the rocks to make the stones in these structures. Many were "recycled" and put to good use elsewhere. There are layers of rock chips underneath the plaza between the Royal Residence and the Temple of the Condor to provide drainage and stabilization. (See "Various Sights on the Way Out.") Incidentally, the finest example of a bronze casting found by Bingham was here in the Serpent Rock area. It is a knife, 5½ inches (13 cm.) long, featuring a fisherman hauling in a fish (Fig. 51).

Figure 50. Rock with natural fractures

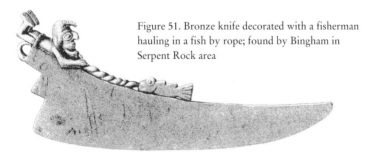

Figure 51. Bronze knife decorated with a fisherman hauling in a fish by rope; found by Bingham in Serpent Rock area

The Sacred Plaza (Conjunto 4)

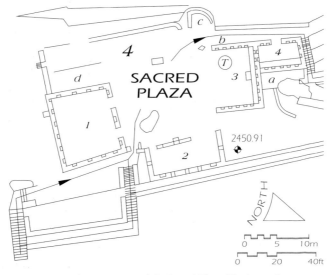

Figure 52. Map of the Sacred Plaza (Conjunto 4)

Now proceed north to the Sacred Plaza. With major buildings on three sides of a large central plaza, it is the most significant of the ceremonial areas. On the fourth open side you can look down the precipitous slope to the Urubamba River below and across the valley to the San Miguel Range. Also on this side is a semicircular foundation wall ("c" in Fig. 52) said to face the same direction as the great semicircular wall of the Coricancha in Cusco. It may be a viewing platform or partial foundation of a new temple on the western side of the plaza.

Our investigations during 2001 and 2002 were focused in part on "unfinished construction," that is, aspects of Machu Picchu that were never finished due to the Spanish invasion and conquest of the Inca Empire. We will point out these features as you go along. They teach us about the architecture, the methodology of

Figure 53. Temple of the Three Windows with enormous polygonal stones, which looks down on the Main Plaza

construction, and the use of manpower. They also help bring Machu Picchu to life as you imagine engineers and stonemasons picking up their tools, abandoning their work, and going home, eventually realizing that their rulers would never come back to this royal estate. The Sacred Plaza was definitely a work in process.

On the eastern side lies the Temple of the Three Windows. The windows are exceptionally large and look down upon the Main Plaza, the Eastern Urban Sector and the mountains beyond (Fig. 53). Polygonal (many-sided) stones of awesome size and shape, exquisitely fitted, make up its walls and windows (Fig. 54). Originally there were five windows, the two outer ones later closed off to form niches. Many sherds were found beneath the windows, perhaps indicating ritualistic breaking of ceremonial pots and *keros* (drinking cups). The partially completed gables at both ends, along with the protruding round pegs, indicate that this temple was going to be roofed. A wooden beam spanning the front would have been supported by the receptacles in the side walls and by the central upright stone. A small stepped stone next to the upright stone may symbolize a mountain (Fig. 55). There is a similar stone at the temple at Pisac. Now take a look at the northwest corner of the north wall. There is a groove run-

Figure 54. Temple of the Three Windows with rock "in transit." Arrow points to groove for corner delineation.

Figure 55. Small stepped stone in the Temple of the Three Windows may symbolize a mountain

ning the full height of the wall which marks the desired corner. Stone masons would have hammerstoned the north wall down to that groove.

The Principal Temple (Building 3) on the north side has several enormous stones composing its lower walls, with upper rows of rectangular stones diminishing in height and creating niches at different levels (Fig. 56). None of these niches is at an easily accessible height, indicating perhaps that they were designed to hold fragile or ceremonial objects. Here again, there are cuts in the side walls to hold a beam across the front of the building; however, the upper rows of stones do not form the usual triangular gables for supporting a thatched roof, and they are superbly

Figure 56. East wall of the Principal Temple settled during Inca times

crafted and fitted. Because of inadequate preparation of the foundation at the time of construction (unusual, considering the superb foundations elsewhere), the east wall has settled. This has caused it to tilt outward, pulling with it a part of the rear wall, remarkably without disturbing the arrangement of the stones. Most of the settlement occurred in Inca times and probably caused construction to cease. The side walls would probably have continued upward, forming a *wayrona*-style building, albeit much larger than any other at Machu Picchu. A huge altar-like stone sits along the back wall. Bingham surmised that royal mummies may have been worshipped there. To examine Inca construction techniques, look at the tilting wall from the outside, where it meets the back wall (Fig. 57). You can see that the stones were placed and fitted first; then they would have been hammered down to form a corner. Figure 57 also shows an unusual cut stone in the back wall that no one has yet explained.

Building 1 in Figure 52 is of ordinary construction and appears to have been purely utilitarian. However, it was likely plastered and painted for a finished look. Some of the pegs are made of

Figure 57. Unfinished corner of the tilting wall of the Principal Temple, with unusual cut stone, viewed from outside

Figure 58. Building 1, with one wall covering part of a niche

pink granite, which usually is not found in Machu Picchu. In the right back corner a change in construction can be noted: the wall covers part of the niche, certainly not part of the original design (Fig. 58). These sorts of anomalies reveal the human touch and help bring Machu Picchu to life.

Figure 59. Highly polished triangular stone near western wall of the Principal Temple

Figure 60. One wall of the Sacristy is polygonal with thirty-two angles

Three stones in the plaza are worth mentioning. One is a large oblong stone considered "in transit." Note the stones underneath the rock like crude roller bearings, a technique the Inca used to move heavy objects (Fig. 54, page 46). It is possible that this rock was destined to be the central upright stone supporting the beam across the front of the Principal Temple. The second stone is an altar-like stone near the center of the plaza, and the third is a highly polished angled stone near the western wall of the Principal Temple (Fig. 59). One side of this stone is being scratched by guides who use their sticks to indicate that the stone seems to point to the Southern Cross. These are "worked" stones and would have had some significant purpose, now lost to us.

Behind and attached to the Principal Temple on the northern side is a small but exquisite room (No. 4 in Fig. 52) sometimes called the Sacristy. It has a row of small, perfectly uniform niches and a stone "couch" along the back wall. A remarkable polygonal stone with thirty-two angles makes up one wall, as if the stonemasons were showing their unlimited capabilities (Fig. 60). But note also that the stone is unfinished. The most obvious feature is the left niche, which does not match the niche on its right.

The Intiwatana (Conjunto 5)

Figure 61. Map of Intiwatana (Conjunto 5)

From the Sacred Plaza, go to the west side of the Principal Temple and past the Sacristy to the impressive and high-quality series of staircases that lead up to the Intiwatana (Fig. 62). The stairway alone tells you that you are approaching a site of major significance. Each stair is a separate but matching block of granite. At the head of these stairs is another horizontal ring, much smaller than the one in the Royal Residence (Fig. 63), which could also have held a torch or royal staff. Then go up to a platform with a three-sided building (No. 1 in Fig. 61) on the west. Note how the Inca transformed a door into a window (Fig. 64). On the east side of this platform are Machu Picchu's best "image stones" or "echo stones," seemingly representing the triangular peaks of

Figure 62. The Intiwatana Pyramid

52

Figure 63. Small horizontal ring resembling that found in the Royal Residence

ring →

Figure 64. The Inca filled in this door to create a window

Mount Yanantin, and the right one the close, rounded top of Putucusi Mountain (Fig. 65). There are other "image stones" at Machu Picchu and other Inca sites. Perhaps these man-altered stones were intended to create a ritual connection with the mountains and their gods.

From here you get the classic view of the Intiwatana stone. Two sets of stairs carved out of the *in situ* rock (also called

Figure 65. Image stones representing Mount Yanantin and Putucusi

Figure 66. Intiwatana platform, the highest point in the urban area

natural rock formation or living rock) lead to the final platform, the highest point in the urban area and the site of the famous Intiwatana stone (Fig. 66). The Intiwatana was sculpted from the rock that formed the peak of this natural pyramid, creating an elegant and multifaceted stone masterpiece of exceptional elegance and beauty (Fig. 67). Hiram Bingham mistakenly named it the Intiwatana, meaning "the place to which the sun was tied" in the Quechua language. Since the Intiwatana is such a famous stone, an explanation of its name is in order. Dr. John Rowe, the leading authority on the Inca, writes:

> There is a building in Pisac that surrounds a rock outcrop the top of which was cut down by the Incas so as to end up as a circular protuberance rising from a flat stone table. The stone protuberance at Pisac is traditionally called "Intihuatana" by the local people, and the American E. G. Squier decided that it was a gnomon or a sort of sundial that would cast its shadow on the flat table around it. Bingham decided that the stone at Machu Picchu with a more or less vertical

Figure 67. Intiwatana stone, not a sundial but sometimes called "the place to which the sun was tied"

protuberance at the top was a gnomon, and he borrowed the name of the Pisac one for it. The comparison is bad. The Machu Picchu stone is four sided, and the base from which it rises is not flat. The Incas did not use gnomons for solar observation; they looked at the horizon to see where the sun rose and set. Max Uhle, who was a better archaeologist than Squier, studied the Pisac protuberance and concluded that it would not cast a useful shadow. The name "Intihuatana" is not ancient and is not recorded until the 19th century.

We can say, however, that this beautiful sculpture, the pinnacle of a natural pyramid, with views of all of the holy mountains, was undoubtedly involved in religious ceremonies of the highest order. Anthropologist and author Johan Reinhard, discoverer of the famous mummified Inca Maiden atop one of Peru's highest peaks, argues convincingly that the Intiwatana stone is associated with mountain worship. He points out that taking the left (western) steps up to the platform puts the Intiwatana in direct

Figure 68. Intiwatana replicating Huayna Picchu (in background) in an abstract way

juxtaposition with Huayna Picchu, replicating its shape and shadows in an abstract way (Fig. 68). He points out that geographically the Intiwatana is at a central point from which sacred mountains were in alignment with the cardinal directions and where significant celestial activity took place. Also notice the flat stone near the left (western) steps, which is carved with a V-shaped depression, creating an "arrow" pointing south (Fig. 69). At the top of Huayna Picchu there is another similar south-pointing stone. Visible to the south from Huayna Picchu is Salcantay, one of the mountains most revered by the Inca. You will see two more arrow stones in the Eastern Sector, also pointing south. In any case, if possible, visit this inspiring place late in the afternoon when the shadows are long and the colors are warm.

From here you can absorb breathtaking views in all directions with extraordinary vertical relief. To the south is Machu Picchu Mountain, to the west is the San Miguel Mountain Range, and to the north is Huayna Picchu with the smaller Uña Picchu on its left. Then, to the east, the entire Eastern Urban Sector lies before you. From left to right, you can see the *wayronas* and the Sacred Rock; a group of unusual, upright, jagged rocks at the top of a large set of terraces (the Unfinished Temple) (Fig. 70); the impressive three symmetrical double-jamb doorways; a grand staircase; the beautiful Artisans' Wall; and the Temple of the Condor.

Directly below is the Main Plaza, which separates the *hanan* (higher) area from the *hurin* (lower) area, a tradition in Inca city planning. At Machu Picchu, the Western Sector is the *hanan*, the Eastern is the *hurin* area. The plaza was also a great expanse for gatherings and ceremonies. The flat terraces adjacent to it may have been viewing platforms. The stone in the center of the plaza has been the subject of debate. Did it lie flat as now, or did it stand upright? Since the Inca had no tradition of statuary in the center of plazas as Western countries do, the stone probably lay flat. Excavations around it have unearthed nothing. Its significance, if any, is unknown.

Figure 69. "Arrow stone" pointing south, near western steps of the Intiwatana

Figure 70. The Unfinished Temple, with its upright, jagged rocks topping a set of large terraces

The Eastern
Urban Sector

The best route through the Eastern Sector is not as direct or obvious as in the Western Sector. First you will go to the Sacred Rock area, and then you can head south either by the short and bumpy trail along the eastern side of Peripheral Area C to Conjuntos 7 and 8, or south through the Main Plaza all the way to the ramp between Conjuntos 16 and 17. Or, if you are coming from the south, you would be starting with Conjunto 16 or 17. In any case, the following descriptions will be identified by conjunto number, and you can simply choose whichever route you wish. The red lines on the foldout map represent the routes so that you will not get lost in the maze. The following route is one option.

The Sacred Rock
(Conjunto 6), the Unfinished
Temple, and the Petroglyph
(Peripheral Area C)

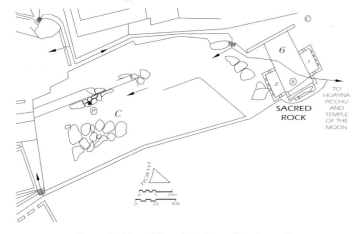

Figure 71. Map of Sacred Rock area (Conjunto 6)

From the Intiwatana, head north and down a long granite staircase to the Main Plaza. Looking back at the natural pyramid, you
can appreciate the steep, narrow terraces built on this side, both
for erosion control and for some specialty crops, perhaps herbs
and flowers. Then cut across the Plaza to the Sacred Rock complex. The centerpiece, the 25-foot-long rock, sits up on its own
pedestal, flanked by two *wayronas*. Looking to the east, notice
that the shape of this rock resembles Mount Yanantin in the
background (Fig. 72).

Coauthor Dr. Valencia excavated and restored the Sacred Rock
complex many years ago and published his findings, wherein he
provided a drawing showing the method of creating stable foundations to last for centuries (Fig. 73). It reminds us of the massive

Figure 72. Sacred Rock, flanked by *wayronas*, resembles Mount Yanantin in background

Figure 73. Sketch of *wayrona* and foundations, showing how foundations were created to last for centuries

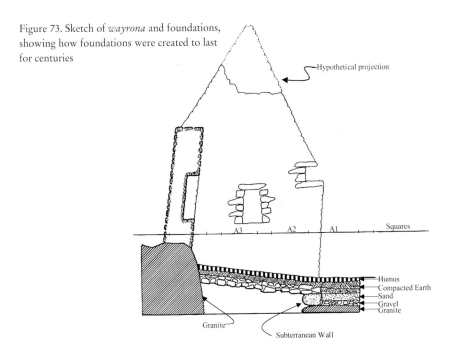

Hypothetical projection

A3   A2   A1   Squares

Humus
Compacted Earth
Sand
Gravel
Granite

Granite

Subterranean Wall

effort needed throughout Machu Picchu to create buildable sites on such difficult terrain. You will find the reconstructed *wayrona* thatched-roof details of special interest. Behind the south *wayrona* is a large rock with a groove cut into it (Fig. 74), used for collecting and diverting water that dripped from the roof. This indicates that the Inca roof thatch was much thicker than the reconstructed roof thatch. This would have required a different structural support for the heavy roof, as proposed by architect Vince Lee (Fig. 74a). This is the roof structure we recommended to the *National Geographic* magazine artist to use in his cutaway of the storehouse. (See painting on back side of the fold-out map at end of book.) In any case, the roof drip line demonstrates the extraordinary detail used by the Inca to handle drainage water.

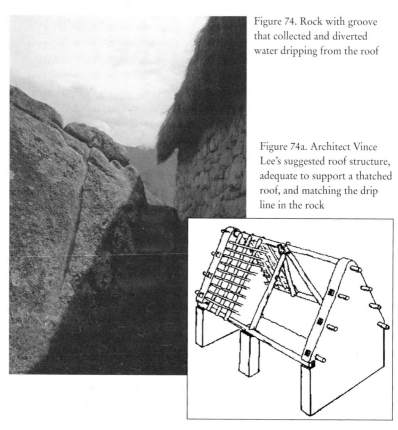

Figure 74. Rock with groove that collected and diverted water dripping from the roof

Figure 74a. Architect Vince Lee's suggested roof structure, adequate to support a thatched roof, and matching the drip line in the rock

Figure 75. Route up to the platform of the Unfinished Temple to the left of the partially constructed wall

Now if you have time for a little side trip, go south to Peripheral Area C, the terraced mound with the huge, upward-jutting, jagged rocks you saw from the Intiwatana (Fig. 70, page 58). Take the dirt trail south of Conjunto 6 and scramble up to the left of the stones shown in Figure 75. Note that the large stones form the beginnings of a wall. This takes you directly onto the highest terrace above the Main Plaza. Continue south along the western edge of the terrace. About halfway along this terrace on the right is a low, flat rock with many cracks (Fig. 76). A small petroglyph is incised onto its surface. It lies horizontally, like the Serpent Rock petroglyphs in the Quarry (Fig. 77). Roughly 14 inches in diameter, it consists of a central point from which sixteen lines radiate. Unfortunately, someone has enlarged the central point, revealing white granite, and making it visually more difficult to see the slender emanating lines. The heavier lines form four right angles, and between these are three thinner lines. Some say it resembles the Inca *ceque* system of Cusco, the imaginary lines radiating from the center of Cusco to various *huacas*, or sacred places. The petroglyph was recorded and photographed by

Figure 76. Large, flat, cracked rock with petroglyph

Figure 77. Detail of petroglyph with sixteen radiating lines; some say it resembles the *ceque* system of Cusco

Figure 78. Construction ramp for dragging stones to the next terrace of the Unfinished Temple

Bingham and is of Inca origin. With the unlimited capabilities of Inca stonemasons, one wonders why these petroglyphs look like scratches rather than fully developed carvings.

A walk on top of this mound, with its strange capricious pinnacles and its cut-but-unfinished stones, evokes feelings of discovery. Excavations and examinations of the site in 2001 revealed Inca construction methods, hammerstones in various sizes, and tiny offerings. It appears to be an unfinished temple in a very early stage of construction. Return the way you came, but now go onto the terrace just below the one you were on. Here is a crude construction ramp of earth and rocks that would have been used for dragging stones up to the next terrace (Fig. 78).

This complex marks the northern end of the urban area and the beginning of another natural and archaeological environment, Huayna Picchu Mountain with its terraces and ceremonial structures. From behind the Sacred Rock, trails lead to Huayna Picchu and to the Temple of the Moon. (See "Side Trip: Huayna Picchu, including Uña Picchu and Alternate Trail to the Temple of the Moon" and "Side Trip: Temple of the Moon.")

Conjuntos 7 and 8 and the Unfinished Wall

Figure 79. Map of Conjuntos 7 and 8

There is a short, rocky, but manageable trail that begins just behind the Sacred Rock on the east side of Peripheral Area C. The retaining wall along this trail is made of huge boulders that were left unfinished. The sequence of construction was that the rocks were placed first, then were hammered down to a straighter and smoother surface. A short walk takes you to the back entrance of Conjunto 7. This enclosure had special status because its front entrance is a double-jamb doorway. Another explanation, however, is that since the doorway faced the Main Plaza, for aesthetic reasons it was made to match the three doorways of Conjunto 9. There is also the tiniest of "mortars" in No. 1. It has the same characteristics as the "mortars" in Conjunto 16—that is, a bowl carved into an *in situ* rock. Its purpose is unknown. In front of the "mortar" is a long rock; the stones underneath it indicate that it was "in transit." Angle through the conjunto and exit through the double-jamb doorway. Turn right to see the massive wall (this is the south wall of Peripheral Area C). Some people see the shape of a bird about 15 feet long: beak, head, body and tail feathers formed by the placement of stones, with perhaps another small "baby" bird on its head (Figs. 80 and 81). Others say the perceived figure is merely due to random stone placement.

Turn around and head left down the path to the single entrance of Conjunto 8. The arrangement, with just three rooms and a large uncovered patio, allows a concentration of people and may indicate that some handicraft activity took place here.

Figure 80. Massive south wall of Peripheral Area C; some see the shape of a bird in the stones

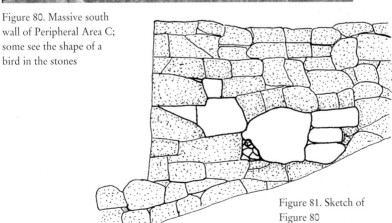

Figure 81. Sketch of Figure 80

The Three Doorways
(Conjunto 9)
and the Artisans' Wall

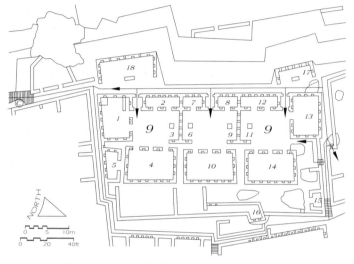

Figure 82. Map of the Three Doorways (Conjunto 9)

From the entrance of Conjunto 8 it is a very short distance to the service entrance of Conjunto 9. As you can see from the floor plan, Conjunto 9 has three units of unusual symmetry with matching walls, doorways and even niches. Each of these units, though not completely separated from each other, has a double-jamb doorway to the path overlooking the Main Plaza, suggesting elite residents, perhaps members of the royal Inca's clan. Dr. Richard Burger, Curator of Anthropology at Yale University's Peabody Museum, describes them thus: "We can immediately identify a sector of high-status households. In the classic form, called *kancha* by the Inca themselves, rectangular buildings used for sleeping, cooking and household storage were arranged within a walled compound around a central patio. Each *kancha* group has a single entrance, and would have been used by a single group. Bingham, aware of Inca custom, correctly identified these as *ayllu* households." (*Ayllu* means "kinship group.") This interpretation is reinforced by the location of two *wayrona*-type buildings (17 and 18), facing the path, which could have provided security and controlled access to the three doorways.

From the path there is a fine view — from right to left (north to south) you can see Huayna Picchu Mountain, the smaller Uña Picchu Mountain, the Intiwatana, the Temple of the Three Windows, the Quarry, the Royal Residence, the Temple of the Sun, the Agricultural Sector, and the Guardhouse, with Machu Picchu Mountain in the background. As you continue south on the path, just before you go down the long staircase, there is a small terrace to the south of Building 18. The rock at the edge appears to be another image rock (Fig. 83).

A grand staircase takes you down to the so-called Artisans' Wall, which has some of the finest stonework in Machu Picchu (Fig. 84). Instead of the coursed masonry of "the most beautiful

Figure 83. Image rock near Building 18

Figure 84. Artisans' Wall, some of the finest stonework at Machu Picchu

Figure 85. Drainage hole in Artisans' Wall

wall," here each stone has a different shape, cut and fitted with utmost care and intricacy, forming an exquisite mosaic. And instead of gray, the wall has a warm, salmon-colored tone. Also note the drain hole built into the wall (Fig. 85). It indicates the floor level of the conjunto on the other side of the wall and shows remarkable advance planning during the wall's construction. The portion of the wall below the drainage hole, therefore, is a retaining wall. This is just one of about 130 such drainage holes for handling rainwater in this climate of 77 inches of annual rainfall, and another indication of the meticulous engineering that produced this remarkable site.

Group of the Mortars
(Conjuntos 14, 15, and 16)

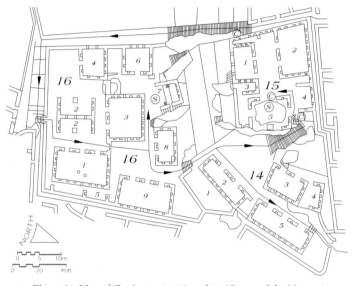

Figure 86. Map of Conjuntos 14, 15, and 16 (Group of the Mortars)

The Group of the Mortars is represented by three conjuntos, numbered 14, 15 and 16, within its identifying walls. Access is from either a double-jamb doorway on the south, or a narrow path on the north. The north access is quite crude and might be thought of as a non-Inca "breakthrough"; however, a cut stepping stone indicates that this was a "back door" in Inca times. We will take the "front door." At the south end of the Artisans' Wall, take the left ramp heading east and up to the double-jamb doorway on the left. Only the lower portions remain, but from the inside you can see how the barholds were integrated into the walls (Fig. 87). For the barhold on the left, the sides, bottom and bar were all carved from one rock. Looking back out to the ramp, notice that a decision was made by the Inca to have a wider

Figure 87. Barholds inside the double-jamb doorway to Conjunto 16; the indentation in the threshold rock at the right wall shows the Inca decided on a wider doorway than originally planned.

doorway. There is an indentation in the threshold rock where the wall on the right was originally to be placed (Fig. 87). It also shows how the Inca fitted rocks for greater stability.

The first, Conjunto 16, is called the Group of the Mortars because of the two "mortars" (Fig. 88) (as in mortar and pestle for grinding grain; however, a more appropriate term would have been grinding stone, used with a rocker) carved in rocks on the floor of the building on the immediate right (No. 1 in Fig. 86). A photograph by Bingham shows what could have been a rocker found near the "mortars" (Fig. 89). The purpose and significance of the building and its stones are still being debated. Some have suggested an astronomical purpose because, when water is standing in the "mortars," the sky is reflected there. This theory assumes the building had no roof. While the debate goes on, the current consensus is that the building did not have a roof. Therefore, you will note on the *National Geographic* magazine's rendition of Machu Picchu that the Building of the Mortars has no

Figure 88. Two "mortars" in the Group of the Mortars; their purpose is still unknown

Figure 89. Photo by Bingham of "mortars" with boy holding "rocker"

roof. Another structure of interest is No. 2, facing the "mortars" building. It is made of back-to-back *wayronas* with exceptionally high and steep gables.

Continue through the second double-jamb doorway. Notice that the barholds on either side are perpendicular to each other rather than straight across, and one of them has no bar. This suggests that a pole or other stiff object was placed in the barless opening and tied to the bar on the other side of the doorway

Figure 90. Barholds perpendicular to each other indicate the use of a pole between the barholds

Figure 91. Stagelike shrine with different styles of stonework

(Fig. 90). Around to the left is a stagelike shrine (No. 7 in Fig. 86). There is even a "stage-door" opening on the right (Fig. 91). Interestingly, the lower left wall is made of carefully fitted stones, while the other walls are of crude stonework. These walls were likely plastered and painted. On both sides, the narrowest of stairways lead to a terrace behind the shrine. On the southwest corner of that terrace is another carved, arrowlike stone, like the ones at the Intiwatana and on the peak of Huayna Picchu, again apparently pointing south toward Salcantay Mountain (Fig. 92). There is a similar arrow carving on the fourth step of a stairway to the right of the shrine (Fig. 93).

Retrace your steps and continue north up a staircase with a banister that was ingeniously cut out of the *in situ* rock (Fig. 94). Now you are in Conjunto 14. Here you see a large patio and a grand staircase curving up to Conjunto 15 (Fig. 95). Near the top of the staircase is a small opening with a large cavern below, from which you can sometimes feel air flowing. Another such hole is

Figure 92. Above stagelike shrine, arrow-shaped stone (lower center) points south to Salcantay Mountain

Figure 93. Four steps with arrow stone on top step pointing south

at the top of the staircase just around the corner to the left (Fig. 96). One can only imagine the foundation work required to build this higher level of structures on such a jumble of rocks. Next to the upper hole is another shrine—a large carved natural rock with partial walls setting it off.

Go back down the staircase and turn north (left), then walk between Buildings 3 and 5 of Conjunto 14 and exit through the narrow "back door" described above.

Figure 94. Staircase with banister cut from *in situ* rock, leading up to Conjunto 14

Figure 95. Grand curving staircase up to Conjunto 15

78

From the vicinity of the Guardhouse, and with its nearly white granite walls and thatched roofs, Machu Picchu sparkled in the morning as seen on June 21, 1530. The Inca are celebrating the Winter Solstice.

Some 470 years later, the royal estate has retained much of its original grandeur. This photo, which was used by the National Geographic artist, provided the basis for the magazine's May 2002 reconstruction painting.

The llama train loaded with goods passes through the Main Gate of Machu Picchu on its way to the grain storehouse on the right, into Conjunto 1.

Llamas still wander through the Main Gate as in Inca times, even though the farmers are long gone.

The gabled roofs of Conjunto 1, just beyond the urban wall and long stairway, provided good shelter against the frequent rains. The upright stone on the lower left was a survey stone.

The penthouse-like tower of Conjunto 17 added a unique architectural contrast to the two-story building that served the Temple of the Condor. The guinea pig hutches are built into the walls of the lower floor.

Even now, the Temple of the Condor retains its intricate and complex features that provide visitors with a special exploratory experience.

Just beyond the Main Gate in Conjunto 1, the llamas are delivering their goods and then taking the steps up to the pens on the left. The cutaway of the storehouse shows both the upper and lower floors and a roof structure that could support the heavy thatched roof.

Today visitors passing through the Main Gate can appreciate the comprehensive city planning at Machu Picchu, which provided for the needs of the Inca, their guests, and the supporting community.

The Temple of the Sun with its conical roof is a Machu Picchu focal point, with the finest stonework in Peru. The Inca guards provided tight security for this most private of temples.

Today the temple (also known as the Torreon) still inspires awe with its carved rocks surrounded and protected by the curved wall and the sculpted stone at the entrance to the royal tomb below.

The great plaza separating the eastern and western urban sectors provided a huge square for festivities such as this one, on June 21, 1530.

Then, as now, the broad green swath provided the only large flat open space in Machu Picchu. The dense urban sectors on both sides rise fairly steeply and are laced with stairs and paths.

The sea of golden thatched roofs serve to highlight the many buildings of Machu Picchu and to focus attention on the unroofed Building of the Mortars on the right.

In modern times visitors can only imagine the bustle of activity at Machu Picchu, especially when the Inca ruler and his entourage would be there, swelling the population to perhaps 1,000.

In early times the Inca Canal crossed the moat as an aqueduct. Here, a llama train passes in the foreground. The orchid is one of 400 varieties found in the Machu Picchu sanctuary.

The Inca built for the ages. The walls, the buildings, the stone stairs, and the paths are mostly still there—only the roofs are missing. And if you listen carefully, perhaps you will even hear the llamas with bells on their ears, bringing produce to the city.

Note the tree in the present-day photo. This is where the gold bracelet was found propped up against a buried Inca wall. In the painting, the wall is undoubtedly already buried and its treasure forgotten.

Thousands of stone chips left over from hammerstoning the building blocks of Machu Picchu are also buried under the grass, providing underground drainage that moved rainwater off site.

In the upper center, on a series of very large terraces, are some great upright jagged rocks. Here the Inca were building another temple as evidenced by construction ramps and walls.

Machu Picchu was abandoned while construction was still in its early stages. We now call it the Terrace of the Unfinished Temple.

Here, on June 21, 1530, the Intiwatana Pyramid is used by Inca priests in a religious ceremony with hundreds of participants in the plaza below. Even in Inca times, the Principle Temple was unfinished because of the settlement of the east wall.

The stillness of Machu Picchu today is in stark contrast to the hustle of activity in its golden years. The Principle Temple still bears the burden of the east wall settlement, but the two wayronas of the Sacred Rock have been reroofed.

Artists of the Cusco School, commissioned to paint "The Last Supper" by the Spanish Conquistadors, used the traditional roasted Inca guinea pig as the centerpiece in front of Christ. The huge painting is displayed in the Cathedral in the main square in Cusco.

Figure 96. Hole at top of staircase and at foot of shrine

Conjuntos 10 and 11

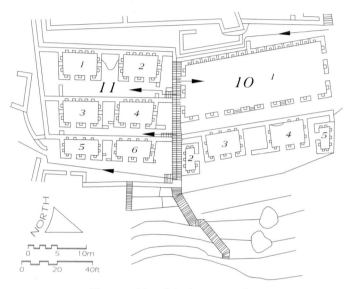

Figure 97. Map of Conjuntos 10 and 11

Leaving Conjunto 14 through the rear exit, you are at Conjunto 11, a part of Machu Picchu's support infrastructure. It consists of six two-storied, symmetrical *qolqas* (storehouses), conveniently located along the staircase that led both up to the elite residential area (Conjunto 9) and down to the lower agricultural terraces, now cut off by the dense forest. The continuation of the trail was discovered in 1996–1998 but remains inaccessible. See "Recently Discovered Inca Trail Down to the Urubamba River." Go up the stairway to see how easily both the lower and upper floors of the *qolqas* could be accessed. There are windows in the gables of the second story that were

Figure 98. *Kallanka* (great hall) in Conjunto 10

part of a ventilation system designed to help preserve the agricultural products. Access to Conjunto 10 is also from these stairs, immediately to the north. Building 1, with its twelve entrances, was another *kallanka* like the one up near the Guardhouse. Adjacent to it is a large open patio. This *kallanka* and patio were used by the people who resided and/or worked in the urban area (Fig. 98). The *kallanka* is under reconstruction.

Conjunto 12

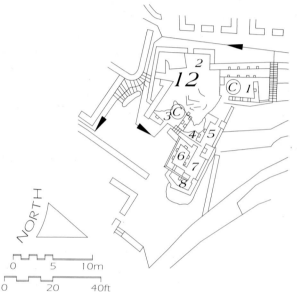

Figure 99. Map and details of Conjunto 12

Conjunto 12, with its multiple levels and small caves, is the smallest and most intricate conjunto at Machu Picchu. To get there, go back down the stairs and head south. Immediately east of Conjunto 11 and overlooking the Urubamba Valley is Conjunto 12's dominant feature, a beautifully carved natural rock with a seat and, on its edge, three small protrusions that seem to represent mountains and valleys in miniature (Fig. 100). At the lower level (take the stairs on the south side) there is a cave, a maze of small rooms leading from one to another, and a final small platform with a panoramic view. Expeditions in 1988 uncovered

Figure 100. Carved natural rock shrine overlooking the Urubamba Valley; three small protrusions on the end may represent mountains and valleys

a number of artifacts, the most interesting of which was a small bronze idol found in Room 6, "with a clear representation of the masculine sex." This artifact is now missing. The complex shows the Inca's extraordinary use of the steep slope, the rock formations, and the cave, and appears to have served a ritualistic function.

Conjunto 13 and Intimachay

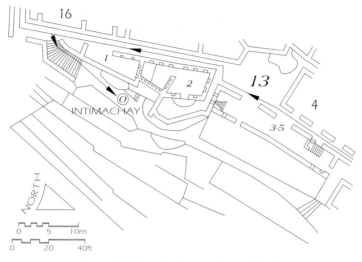

Figure 101. Map of Intimachay, Cave of the Sun

Conjunto 13 is a collection of buildings and rooms whose purposes have not been identified; however, there is a very interesting structure that you can locate in Figure 101 just to the east and downslope of Rooms 1 and 2 of Conjunto 13. In 1984, archaeoastronomer David S. Dearborn and a team investigated an unusual cave and concluded that it served as a solstice observatory. They named it Intimachay, or Cave of the Sun. To reach this unusual cave, take the path between Rooms 4 and 3-5 of Conjunto 13 and continue south. Just before you get to the southeast corner of Conjunto 16, take a sharp left turn; a short staircase leads down to the cave. An arrow points to Intimachay in Figure 101.

Dearborn found that the Inca had altered and embellished the cave in order to admit the rays of the rising sun, coming through a notch in the far mountain ridge, to reach the back wall of the cave at a specific time of the year. The unique tunnel-like window was created by cutting into the natural rock to form the south

N° 076561 **SERIE:** **108**

HABILITADO
S/. 77.00

INSTITUTO NACIONAL DE CULTURA
DIRECCION REGIONAL DE CULTURA CUSCO
P.A.N. MACHUPICCHU
12 JUL 2005
11 JUL. 2005
2005
UTILIZADO

"El Instituto Nacional de Cultura, agradece su aporte que servirá para la conservación y mantenimiento del Patrimonio Cultural de la Humanidad".

Imprenta Amauta S.R.Ltda.
R.U.C. 11469060
Calle Pisteros 282 - Cusco

Figure 102. Intimachay's tunnel-like window, which admitted the sun's rays into the cave during the December solstice

Figure 103. Sketch of skyline across the valley, showing the notch through which the sun's rays passed during the solstice to pierce Intimachay

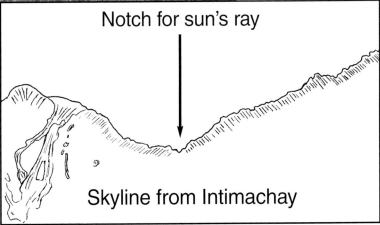

Notch for sun's ray

Skyline from Intimachay

Figure 104. Inca boys of noble
birth wore ear spools upon
their initiation into manhood

wall and bottom, while the north side and top were constructed
of stones (Fig. 102).

Inside the cave a natural rock formation, which descends from
the ceiling, was meticulously squared off at the bottom. The rays
of the rising sun peeking through the notch about 2 miles away
(Fig. 103) would pass through the window and below the hanging rock to the back wall only around the December solstice.
(A flashlight is useful inside the cave, and you can experiment
piercing the window with it from the outside to the back wall.)
In Inca times, Capac Raymi, a feast and ritual during the month
of December, culminated with the initiation of boys of noble
birth into manhood. As they watched the sun rise on the December solstice, their ears were pierced to receive their ear spools
(Fig. 104).

Adjacent to Intimachay on the north is a large overhang. Notice
the cutaway at its edge that directs rainwater straight down rather
than along the underside of the overhang, protecting the area
from rain. Here is a small carved rock creating a seat facing a
niche on the other side.

The Temple of the Condor (Conjunto 17) and Conjunto 18

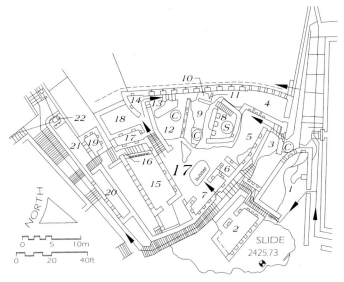

Figure 105. Map of Conjunto 17 (Temple of the Condor)

The Temple of the Condor can be accessed from different directions and doorways. If you happen to be at the lowest of the fountains (Fountain 16 in room 22), continue downhill and then left up the steep staircase to the double-jamb doorway. If you are approaching from the Artisans' Wall, go down the ramp to the east, to the second entrance on the right, which is also a double-jamb doorway indicating an area of very high status. (Avoid the first doorway because it is the back door and may not even have been a doorway in Inca times.)

If you have just been to Intimachay, you will be coming from above. You will pass a large, white, slanting natural rock with a platform cut into its upper end, now called The Slide for obvious reasons (Fig. 106). Its purpose in Inca times is unknown. Take

Figure 106. The Slide, with platform cut into the upper end

Figure 107. Niches in wall, which appear to have served as handholds

Figure 108. Bingham called this the shrine with "Unusual Niches Group"

the stairway below the Slide. Note the four "niches" on the right at descending levels, which are small and do not have the typical trapezoidal shape of other niches at Machu Picchu. They appear to be handholds for the stairway (Fig. 107). Then go up a few steps to the left to the double-jamb doorway directly into Room 7. This is the most dramatic entrance.

You are entering a most fascinating and intricate place. With its fantastic rock formations, grottos and subterranean passageways, the Temple of the Condor is almost theatrical. Here the Inca architects really outdid themselves in using and embellishing the natural formations.

Bingham called this conjunto the "Unusual Niches Group" (Fig. 108) because of the wall with three large niches, built on top of a huge rock (No. 8 in Fig. 105, which also shows it as a shrine). He thought important mummies may have been displayed here and that the holes in the outer corners of each of the niches were used as barholds to tie ropes across the niches to act as barriers. Because of the holes there has been speculation that prisoners were tied and punished here, leading to the name "Prison

Figure 109. Sketch of Andean condor,
South America's largest bird

Figure 110. Temple of
the Condor; the flat,
carved condor rock in
the foreground and the
natural rock "wings"
behind

Figure 111. Inside
stairway of Building
15 is now inaccessible

Group." Now that we know that Machu Picchu was a royal estate and religious center, this theory is highly unlikely. Also note the small niche in the back wall of each of the large niches—another confirmation that this was a shrine.

The condor is South America's largest bird, with a wing span of up to 8 feet and capable of flying to great heights (Fig. 109). It is still revered as a symbol of power and majesty by Andean people today. The stylized condor rock in Conjunto 17 is a flat triangular rock with carved eyes and a beak, and two white semicircular stones creating a "ruff," a characteristic of condors. At the end of the beak is a small hole through which rainwater easily penetrates to gravel and rock below. The condor rock is set off against the rock formations behind it, which form the shape of two outstretched wings, as if the condor were swooping down to catch prey (Fig. 110). "Temple of the Condor" is a very appropriate name.

The temple is complex, with many levels and subterranean caves, making it a great place to explore. Below the right "wing" is a small opening with a few steps leading down. Excavations

Figure 112. Guinea pig hutches built into Building 15's stairway; guinea pigs were and still are roasted for ceremonies and feasts

Figure 113. Fountain 16, accessible only from the Temple of the Condor

by coauthor Valencia and Chicago industrialist and amateur archaeologist James S. Westerman have discovered man-made subterranean passageways, now closed off, that can only be accessed by crawling. You can go under the left "wing," which leads to a cave (No. 13 in Fig. 105) tall enough to stand in, with niches and an entrance on the south side. (Please remove your backpack so you do not scratch the walls.) Or you can enter the cave directly through the south entrance by taking the stairs up and around the south side. There are unexpected views through cavernous openings.

There is a large building on the south side (No. 15 in Fig. 105), whose second floor once could be entered from the condor rock level. An inside stairway, now inaccessible (Fig. 111), leads to the ground floor, where small enclosures for *cuyes* (guinea pigs) were built into the stairway wall (Fig. 112). Ancient guinea pig droppings were found in these hutches. The small edible animal is still considered a delicacy and is served at special occasions and ceremonies. In the cathedral on the main square in Cusco is a large painting of the Last Supper by an Andean artist of the colonial period that shows a roasted guinea pig on the table. (See last photo in second color section.)

The ground floor of Building 15 opens onto a terrace and leads to steps down to Fountain 16. This fountain is the only one that could be accessed only from Conjunto 17 and was therefore private. For additional privacy the water enters the fountain at ground level on the public side of the wall and then makes double turns before falling into a basin (Fig. 113). You can reach this fountain by going back out the double-jamb doorway on the upper side of the conjunto and then taking the steep stairs down on the east side of the conjunto. Much of the privacy wall has crumbled, so you can see the fountain and its double turns.

The easier route out of Conjunto 17 is to take the path (through area 14 in Fig. 105) and the stairs behind the "wings." It takes you closer to the rock with the large niches and along the inside of the wall that forms the western side of the conjunto. The wall has a series of niches and windows. You can then exit by the "back door" and be back on the ramp.

Conjunto 18 is located south of the Temple of the Condor and has been partially restored. It served as another residential area.

Various Sights on the Way Out

The Fountains

If you decided to go down to Fountain 16, you can now work your way up the stairs and look at the individual fountains (Fig. 129, page 109). Fountain 16 is the last in the series along the Stairway of the Fountains and the only private fountain, since it can be accessed only from the Temple of the Condor area. In Inca times the wall surrounding the fountain was much higher, and the low elevation of the entrance from the outside, together with the two jogs the channel makes before discharging its water, would have prevented anyone from seeing inside (Fig. 113, page 92). Starting with Fountain 16, you can backtrack to 15, 14, 13, and so on, appreciating both their common and their unique design. The sight and sound of splashing water must have been as enticing to the Inca as they still are to us. Fountain 10 is unusual in that the water is brought through a small channel in the rock and around to fall into its basin from the opposite direction of the other fountains. At Fountain 7 you join the main north-south path along the eastern edge of Conjuntos 2 and 3 (Temple of the Sun and the Royal Residence).

If, instead, you exited the Temple of the Condor on its north side, you can go up the ramp and over to the same main north-south path.

The Gold Bracelet and Buried Wall

In the plaza between the Royal Residence and the Temple of the Condor is a tree that has become a special landmark. A bit of history is necessary here. The Spanish chroniclers described with awe the exquisite and opulent gold artifacts they saw in Cusco, especially at the Coricancha. They bedazzled the conquistadors, who melted them down and shipped them home to Spain as bullion. We believe the conquistadors never reached Machu Picchu. Surely at this royal retreat and religious center some gold objects graced its temples and holy places as well. Yet during his intensive and exhaustive three years of exploration and excavation at Machu Picchu, Hiram Bingham found no gold.

One explanation is that it was stripped when Inca Atahualpa was captured by the conquistador Pizarro. He promised to spare Atahualpa's life for a ransom: a room filled once with gold and twice with silver. Precious objects flowed in from all over the empire. Machu Picchu, so close to Cusco, would have been a likely source. Another possible explanation is that when the empire and its social structure collapsed, Machu Picchu lost its reason for existence. Objects of value would simply have been taken away as the place was abandoned.

In 1995, as part of its studies of the Inca water supply and agricultural production at Machu Picchu, Wright Water Engineers, an American consulting firm, offered to have soil samples tested at Colorado State University. Under the supervision of Srta. Elva Torres, the Instituto Nacional de Cultura (INC) obtained soil samples from various agricultural terraces and from this plaza just north of the tree. At that location, digging down about 5 feet, a hard object was struck. It was a long-buried Inca wall made of rough stones (Fig. 114), which ran perpendicular to the Condor wall. At the foot of the wall, protected between two small stones, was a bracelet made of gold. If the soil sample had been taken just a few feet north or south, the wall and its unique treasure would not have been found. This discovery instigated a major excavation along the whole wall (Figs. 115 and 116).

The bracelet is made of a rectangular, hammered sheet of 16-carat gold, about 3¼ by 6 inches, curved to fit around the forearm. Two tiny holes on either end were used to fasten the bracelet (Fig. 117). From its location and upright position, it is obvious that it was intentionally placed, perhaps as an offering. But by whom and for what purpose will forever remain a

Figure 114. Recently excavated rough wall where gold bracelet was found

Figure 115. Excavation of the wall shown from above with worker and temporary supports

Figure 116. Excavation of the wall between the Temple of the Condor and the Royal Residence

Figure 117. Gold bracelet discovered at the foot of the excavated rough wall, now on display at the Regional Museum in Cusco

Figure 118. Inca priest model wearing a "gold" bracelet facsimile

Figure 119. Srta. Torres with foundation stones revealed by the excavations; the foundations go much deeper than ground level, helping to explain why Inca architecture has remained so stable

mystery. The bracelet is on display at the Regional Museum in Cusco. A model shows how bracelets like this would have been worn by Inca priests (Fig. 118).

The excavation of the wall also solved another mystery: what happened to the thousands of chips resulting from chipping the rough stones to create the finished stones used in the hundreds of buildings and walls? They not only were used for fill to create the flat surfaces of the plaza, but also provided underdrainage for the 77 inches of rain that fell at Machu Picchu annually. The rainwater would percolate through the grass and soil placed on top of the chips, and then would flow through these permeable chips and the loose-rock wall to run off the urban site in a controlled and harmless fashion.

In Figure 119 Srta. Torres is pointing to the foundation stones that were exposed by the excavations. You can see that the wall goes considerably deeper than ground level, and the wall at the ground level is already a third tier of retaining walls supporting the Royal Residence. This is the kind of foundation preparation that has prevented Machu Picchu from collapsing. The excavation has since been filled in, but you can see where the excavation occurred by comparing the visible wall stones in Figure 120 with the same stones above ground level in Figure 119.

The Water Supply Canals and the Survey Rock

Continue south along the path to the Dry Moat. If you go about one-third of the way up the long staircase between the Dry Moat and the City Wall, you can see where the domestic water supply canal, which feeds the fountains, comes across the agricultural area and through the City Wall. In Figure 121, it is the small canal on the right; the larger canal on the left is a drainage ditch carrying water from the agricultural terraces for discharge into the Dry Moat. You saw this small canal near the uppermost storehouse when you started on the trail to the Guardhouse (Fig. 6, page 7). The water came by gravity flow from springs on Machu Picchu Mountain via a half-mile-long (749-meter) canal. The canal is lined with stone and is about 4 inches deep by 5 inches wide (12 cm by 13 cm). (See "Inca Water Management" and Figs.

Figure 120. Same wall section as in Figure 119 after excavation was filled in

Figure 121. Inca water supply canal across agricultural terraces to City Wall; the wider trench (left) takes runoff from the terraces to the Dry Moat

Figure 122. Carved canal stones for the unfinished canal

127 and 128, pages 107–108.) On a narrow terrace two levels below the one carrying the canal lie a series of stones carved for a second water supply canal (Fig. 122) which was never finished (labeled "Unfinished Canal" on the foldout map). Looking closely at the unfinished stones, you can see how channels were carved into the stones. The master stonemason would cut a groove on both ends of the stone to show width and depth, and then the stonecutter would connect the two (Fig. 123). This canal would have carried much less water than the main canal and looks more like the channels between the fountains. The source of water for this secondary canal would have been a diversion from the main canal. Looking upward you can see the upright rock on the right side of the Dry Moat thought to be a survey marker used for construction purposes (Fig.13, page 13). As you can see, the long staircase you are on provides another route up to the Main Gate and then to the Guardhouse.

Figure 123. Partially carved canal stone; a groove was cut on both ends to indicate width and depth, and then the two were connected by the stonecutter

Agricultural Terraces

From this location you also have a good view of the agricultural terraces and the *qolqas* to the south (Fig. 124). There are hundreds of agricultural terraces at Machu Picchu, not only in the Upper and Lower Agricultural Sectors, but also on the flanks of the Intiwatana pyramid, on both the east and west flanks down to the Urubamba River, and even on the heights of Huayna Picchu. They were carefully constructed for agriculture, drainage, and to prevent erosion of the steep hillsides (Fig. 125). Studies have shown that all these terraces combined would have provided the nutritional requirements for a permanent population of only about 55 people. Experts estimate that there was a permanent population of about 300 people, which swelled to perhaps 1,000 when the royal family, the elite, and their retinue came to visit. Numerous terraces in the vicinity of Machu Picchu and along the fertile floodplain of the Urubamba River, however, provided a sufficient food supply. Because of the special significance of the site, it has been assumed that the terraces in this royal retreat and sacred center were used for specialty crops: corn for the ceremonial beer, or *chicha*, and flowers and herbs. Recently pollen samples from various terraces have been tested and revealed the presence of Zia maize (corn) in most samples, together with a variety of plants that can be used for medicinal purposes.

Adjacent to and just south of the moat is an Inca-period landslide that they tamed and were nearly finished with their corrective measures at the time of abandonment. Look at the unterraced areas where a landslide scarp still exists, the terraces that extend only partially across to the south, and terraces closer to the canal that are of irregular width. Further down, below the main tourist path, some terraces have offset alignments and others have a curve, all due to the earth slippage of about 3 to 6 feet.

To leave the site, take the stairs back down to the path and go through the Lower Agricultural Sector, past the corrals to the storehouses. Exit between the storehouses, the route that many use to enter the site.

Figure 124. Agricultural terraces, *qolqas* (storehouses) and residences for farmers; in the background the location of the Inca Spring, the Inca Trail from Cusco, and Intipunku (Gate of the Sun) are identified

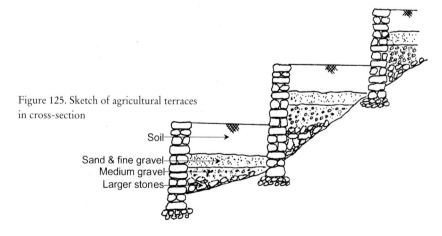

Figure 125. Sketch of agricultural terraces in cross-section

The Mummies

Hiram Bingham named the cave beneath the Temple of the Sun the Royal Mausoleum although no mummies were found there. However, its location under a major temple, the religious importance of caves, its location protected from the elements and from the general populace, its beautifully carved rocks, and its large niches reinforce his interpretation. The Inca fed and clothed their royal mummies, and treated them as if they were simply in a different stage of their existence (Fig. 126). One can imagine the mummy of an important ancestor being placed here

Figure 126. Sketch of mummy being carried by attendants

in preparation for participating in a great ceremony or for giving sage advice. There is even a fine view from inside. Bingham also mentioned two other locations as possible sites to display royal mummies: the great altar of the Principal Temple and the unusual niches in the Temple of the Condor.

The mummies or, realistically speaking, the skeletal remains that Bingham did find were on the outskirts of Machu Picchu, some widely scattered, but most concentrated in three "cemeteries," two on the eastern flanks below Machu Picchu and one on the north slope of Machu Picchu Mountain, 1,000 feet above the Main Gate. Actually, this latter site is along the Inca Trail in a special spot at the foot of a huge rock that juts upward about 50 feet. (See "Side Trip: Intipunku [Gate of the Sun]" and Figs. 143 and 144, page 121) This was the finest burial found by Bingham's team.

Through exhaustive searches by the Indian workers, who were offered generous payments for any finds, the remains of about one hundred seventy individuals were found. Dr. George F. Eaton of Yale University, the supervisor of the burial sites, examined the remains and concluded that the majority were women, though some men and even a few infants were represented. From these findings Eaton, and then Bingham, concluded that Machu Picchu was home to the *aclla* (chosen women), whom the Spanish named the Virgins of the Sun. This myth was perpetuated and even embellished by stories that the *aclla* were whisked away from Cusco at the time of the Spanish invasion to remote Machu Picchu for protection.

All the other data indicated otherwise, however. Most of the burials were crude, the bodies barely protected by rocks from marauding animals, and the artifacts accompanying them were ordinary. Yet the fascinating myth persisted. It has now been put to rest. Dr. Richard L. Burger directed the recent re-analyses of the skeletons now at Yale University's Peabody Museum. They show that the male/female representation is roughly equal, and of the adult females, many had given birth. Nutritional analyses of the bones also revealed that these individuals came from different parts of the empire. Another investigation in the early 1990s by Sonia Guillen, a physical anthropologist, indicated that the bones had shrunk over time, such that these individuals were actually taller than Eaton had surmised. The conclusion is that these were retainers and workers who happened to die on-site.

Why are there so few burials at a site that was occupied for a hundred plus years? Machu Picchu was a royal estate, not a total community. The Inca elite, priests, dignitaries, guests, and entourage would come only for a time, for religious ceremonies and astronomical observations, and perhaps in the winter for the milder climate. If any happened to die on-site, they would probably have been carried back to Cusco for proper death rites. Craftsmen, such as stonemasons, would have been on-site only for a period of time under the *mita* system of temporary service, and then would have returned to their villages. Thus the more permanent population who was keeping the estate in readiness was probably quite small, perhaps three hundred, and many of these people would have rotated back to their homes. Others who may have stayed on, abandoned Machu Picchu in 1572 or shortly thereafter. That year the Spanish Viceroy Toledo ordered a "reduction of the indians." They were forced to move to settlements with churches, such as Ollantaytambo, so the Spaniards could control them more easily.

Inca Water Management

Precipitation during the Inca period of occupation of Machu Picchu is estimated at about 77 inches (1940 millimeters) per year. However, while the Inca were there, the climate was in a dramatic change with annual rainfall increasing as time went on. In the last decade of Machu Picchu ocupation the rainfall was about 83 inches per year (2100 mm/yr), whereas the first decade typically brought about 71 inches per year (1800 mm/yr). As a result, one can say with certainty that Machu Picchu was not abandoned because of a water shortage.

The abundant rainfall also meant that irrigation was not needed for crops at Machu Picchu. This was confirmed during the Wright Water Engineers' field studies: there was no irrigation at Machu Picchu; the natural precipitation was adequate for crop growth from September through May in an average year, and there were no irrigation facilities. The rainfall also meant that natural vegetation flourished in the region with thick lush rain forest—as it still does today. Studies show that precipitation during Inca times closely resembles that of today's climate.

Water management by the Inca was remarkable. At Machu Picchu the planners, engineers, and workmen left a legacy of smart water use. Hiram Bingham noted their technical competence when he reported in *National Geographic* magazine that "the Incas were good engineers."

The most notable water management features at Machu Picchu are below.

The Spring

The spring collection works on the north slope of Machu Picchu Mountain are built on a steep slope to intercept pure groundwater from the 40-acre (16.3-hectare) basin lying above it. The water yield of the spring typically varies from 6 to 30 gallons per minute (25 to 125 liters per minute), depending on the season of the year, and is of excellent quality. The spring is associated with the Machu Picchu Fault, which caused the bedrock to fracture, helping to funnel water to the natural spring. The spring works are a masterpiece of hydrological water development (Fig. 127). Although the spring is a natural phenomenon, its reliable yield is enhanced by the carefully planned and built permeable stone wall set into the steep hillside. (See Fig. 11, page 12, and Fig. 124, page 102, for the location of the spring and the canal.)

The Canal

The Inca Canal is 2,457 feet long (749 meters) with a small cross section, typically only about 4 by 5 inches in size. In a remarkable feat, without modern surveying instruments, the Inca engineers built the canal to be able to carry about 80 gallons (300 liters) per minute by gravity flow on a relatively steady gradient of about 3 percent into Machu Picchu. Had the slope been too steep, the water would have jumped out of the canal; if too shallow, it would

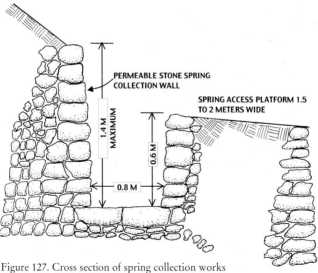

Figure 127. Cross section of spring collection works

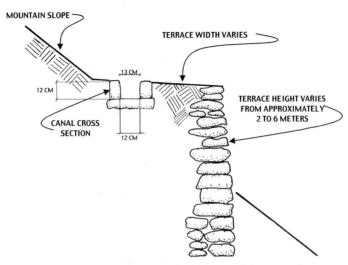

MOUNTAIN SLOPE

TERRACE WIDTH VARIES

13 CM

12 CM

CANAL CROSS
SECTION

12 CM

TERRACE HEIGHT VARIES
FROM APPROXIMATELY
2 TO 6 METERS

Figure 128. Cross section of Inca Canal, which carried about 80 gallons per minute into Machu Picchu by gravity flow

have flowed too slowly to Fountain 1. The canal is lined with rock and built on a terrace formed by a stone retaining wall (Fig. 128). Even though the mountainside is steep and subject to landslides, in 1912 Hiram Bingham found only two areas of canal failure.

The location and elevation of the spring are fixed where the spring exits the side of the mountain. It is likely, therefore, that the planning and layout of the Royal Residence, and even those of the Temple of the Sun, were completed after the spring and the hydraulic slope of the canal were established, so that the purest water at Fountain 1 was available to the Inca ruler and at one of the most important ceremonial sites in Machu Picchu.

The Unfinished Canal

See "Sights on the Way Out: The Water Supply Canals and the Survey Rock," pages 98–100.

The Fountains

The hydraulic focal point of Machu Picchu is the series of sixteen fountains spread out over a vertical fall of 85 feet (26 meters)

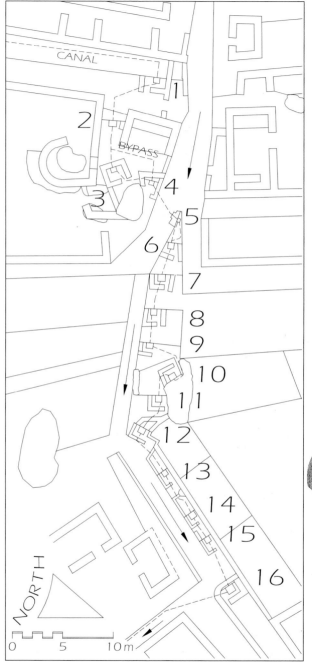

Figure 129. Diagram of the 16 fountains at Machu Picchu, laid out over a vertical fall of 85 feet

CANAL

2

BYPASS

1

4

3

5

6

7

8

9

10

11

12

13

14

15

16

NORTH

0   5   10m

Figure 130. Sketch of *aryballo* (pottery bottle) being carried, using a rope threaded through the handles and over a knob, often in the shape of an animal head

from top to bottom (Fig. 129). The fountains are all similar in design, but each one is unique in detail. Common fountain features are an inlet channel creating a jet of falling water, a stone basin at the bottom, an outlet orifice that could be plugged to fill the basin, and niches (Fig. 24, page 23). Water was collected in pottery bottles known as *aryballos*. Figure 130 shows how the *aryballo* would have been carried. It has handles on either side and a knob, often in the shape of an animal head, over which the rope was strung. The pointed bottom was probably set on a soft floor, permitting the jug to be tilted for pouring. These Inca jugs were famous for their ceramic quality and were used throughout the empire.

Urban Drainage

The ability of the Inca to plan ahead is best illustrated by the urban drainage system containing about 130 outlets, numerous channels, roof drip stones and man-made drainage divides. Outlets were incorporated into walls during construction, not as an afterthought. For example, the drainage holes in the Artisans' Wall were placed at just the right elevation to drain the interior-ground floor levels (Fig. 85, page 70). A well-planned drainage system also serves the entrance to the Royal Residence (Fig. 36, page 31). The Dry Moat, between the Agricultural Sector and the Urban Sector, acts as a main drain, serving both urban and agricultural storm runoff.

The Agricultural Terraces

The soil of the agricultural terraces is rich and productive with good infiltration to avoid runoff. The terrace slopes were kept flat enough to encourage infiltration, and deep underlying permeable zones were constructed to ensure good agricultural drainage (Fig. 125, page 102). The topmost layer may have been the rich soil brought up from the floodplain of the Urubamba River. Vertical surface drains are situated throughout the terrace areas. Any surface runoff was managed to prevent erosion on the steep slopes. Figure 121 (page 99) shows a large lateral drain on the left that would take surface drainage to the Dry Moat. Without excellent drainage many of the terraces would have been subject to collapse and slope failure.

Subsurface Drainage

Without good subsurface drainage, Machu Picchu would be unstable and would have suffered from landslides and soggy ground surfaces. The subsurface drainage system was part of the site preparation. It is estimated that about 60 percent of Machu Picchu construction work was underground to create stable buildable sites. For example, the layer of chipped stones below ground level in the plaza west of the Temple of the Condor provided ample capacity for carrying off surplus groundwater. (See "Sights on the Way Out: Gold Bracelet," page 94.)

Recently Discovered Inca Trail Down to the Urubamba River

After a forest fire on the eastern flank of Machu Picchu in 1969, coauthor Dr. Valencia, then a student, identified an array of terraces and several fountains. These are between Machu Picchu and the river, and north of the Hiram Bingham road (the bus road up to Machu Picchu). The vegetation grew back quickly, the finds were soon enveloped by the thick forest, and his drawings were lost. Then beginning in 1996, the Wright Water Engineers Survey team, for which Dr. Valencia serves as resident archaeologist,

Figure 131. Archaeologists and *macheteros* uncovering and measuring a recently discovered Inca Trail

Figure 132. Recently discovered Inca Trail and terraces on the East Flank, as seen from Huayna Picchu, with Hiram Bingham road in upper left corner

Figure 133. Inca Trail with sturdy wall, terraces, and 9-foot-wide granite steps

113

Figure 134. Coauthor Wright pointing to an inlet channel of one of the fountains designed to cause a jetting of water over the wall

rediscovered the long-lost fountains. In addition they found a portion of a major Inca trail in 1998 with well-constructed retaining walls and several wide granite staircases (Fig. 131). It required extensive clearing by *macheteros* (men wielding machetes) from Aguas Calientes. Figure 132 shows a portion of the cleared trail in a photo taken from Huayna Picchu. Finally, in 1999, the complete Inca Trail to the Urubamba River was discovered.

Getting to and then following the route of this Inca Trail through the dense forest is very difficult because of the steep slope, heavy vegetation, insects and snakes. Beyond the sharp bluff overlooking the Urubamba River, the trail was cleared and

114

Figure 135. Ceremonial fountain was cleaned of debris and made to flow again

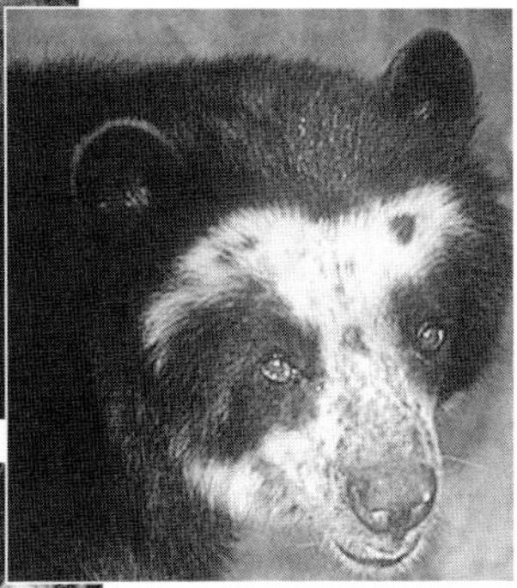

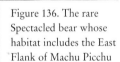

Figure 136. The rare Spectacled bear whose habitat includes the East Flank of Machu Picchu

Figure 137. *Machetero* prays to the holy mountains and Pacha Mama (earth goddess) to keep the water flowing forever

was found to pass by beautiful terraces, ruins of a field house for agricultural workers, fountains, long and narrow side staircases, and places with breathtaking views. The trail itself is typically 6 feet (2 meters) wide with some stairs being 9 feet (3 meters) wide (Fig. 133). Six fountains have been uncovered. Three are utilitarian and would have provided the agricultural workers and travelers with a water supply. Two are ceremonial fountains strategically placed along the trail, which are as beautiful as those adjacent to the Stairway of the Fountains. Coauthor Wright points to the inlet channel of one of the fountains designed to create a jet of water for easy filling of *aryballos* (Fig. 134). The sixth fountain was crushed by a rockfall. The ceremonial fountains offer a grand view of the valley and the dramatic mountains beyond. The water was derived from groundwater flow replenished by rainfall on the slopes above. When cleared of centuries of debris, they flowed again with water clean enough to drink (Fig. 135).

Immediately below the cliffs of Huayna Picchu the trail passes stone retaining walls and crosses ravines until it reaches the river. It represents a great achievement in construction in a seemingly impassable area. The width and quality of the trail, and the accompanying fountains and terraces, indicate that this is the suspected continuation of the main Inca Trail from Cusco. An Inca bridge, which no longer exists, probably took travelers across the Urubamba River. It is expected that the trail will be left to the rain forest because of its steep slopes and important wildlife habitat. The rare and endangered Spectacled bear is shown in Figure 136. One of the team members actually saw and took a photo of one in a tree.

When the 1999 fieldwork was completed, one of the *macheteros* knelt down in prayer, invoking the holy mountains of Machu Picchu, Huayna Picchu and Putucusi, and the earth goddess Pacha Mama, beseeching them to keep the water flowing forever. Then he buried a piece of bread as an offering (Fig. 137).

Side Trips

Inca Drawbridge

There is a subsidiary Inca Trail from Machu Picchu that formerly went around the west side of Machu Picchu Mountain, probably connecting with the main Inca Trail. Now it only leads to what is known as the Inca Drawbridge, the shortest and easiest side trip. You can get there from the Guardhouse in about twenty minutes.

From Peripheral Area F (the Guardhouse and Terrace of the Ceremonial Rock), take the trail indicated on the foldout map by a red arrow pointing to "Inca Trail to Drawbridge." Though it is an easy walk, be careful because there are steep drop-offs. When you come to a barrier, take it seriously and venture no farther. From there you have a good view of the "bridge," an ingenious rock wall protruding from the face of the sheer, 1,000-foot cliff of the Machu Picchu Fault, with a strategic gap (Figs. 138 and 139). There are timbers across the gap, as in the past — Inca security guards could simply remove them to make this route to Machu Picchu virtually inaccessible. The "flying steps" on the wall may have been for construction access. In any case, an unwanted visitor coming up those steps would easily have been rebuffed.

Figure 138. Inca Drawbridge on side of cliff, a twenty-minute walk from the Guardhouse

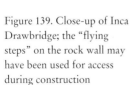

Figure 139. Close-up of Inca Drawbridge; the "flying steps" on the rock wall may have been used for access during construction

Intipunku (Gate of the Sun)

If you look up at Machu Picchu Mountain and then let your eyes follow the ridge down to the first notch, you will see tiny structures in the notch. That is Intipunku (Gate of the Sun). Intipunku served as an important checkpoint along the Inca Trail for traffic control. It is where long-ago visitors got their first view of Machu Picchu (Fig. 3, page 3) and where modern trekkers first see the royal estate in all its glory. At times the mists rise from the Urubamba River, creating a city in the clouds, or the sunrise bathes it in golden light. Here porters in their colorful ponchos may rest before their final plunge down to Machu Picchu (Fig. 140). Sometimes you can watch them thundering down with their

Figure 140. Intipunku (Gate of the Sun) with porters, on the way down to Machu Picchu

Figure 141. One of the porters, just above the shrine on the Inca Trail

Figure 142. Resident llamas on the agricultural terraces at Machu Picchu

unbelievable burdens of camping gear and tables for trekkers on the Inca Trail. Consider them the descendants of the *chasqui*, the famous runners who delivered messages along the vast network of roads that connected the sprawling Inca empire (Fig. 141).

This is a fairly easy roundtrip hike of about two to three hours. You will want to have time to investigate the structures along the way and up at Intipunku. Bring along some water. From just below the Guardhouse stairs, start up a long ramp with the upper agricultural terraces on your right, where resident llamas often congregate (Fig. 142). The ramp becomes mostly a stone trail between a retaining wall and the valley. The entire way to Intipunku is a ramp with some stairs, not too strenuous, an obvious rise in elevation, and a distance of about 1¼ miles (2 kilometers). Be conscious that you are treading on the famous Inca Trail, the road from Cusco.

Figure 143. Fifty-foot rock arching toward the Inca Trail, site of the third "cemetery" found by Bingham's team

Figure 144. Close up of rock along Inca Trail, site of the finest grave found at Machu Picchu, No. 26

Figure 145. Eaton's sketch of cemetery in front of huge rock

Figure 146. The finest burial (No. 26) found at the base of the overhanging rock along the Inca Trail. Note the pottery and the skeleton of a dog buried with its master.

Figure 147. Compare with Figure 146. This is a detailed sketch of the pot on the right in Burial 26. It is decorated with a human face, partly in relief and partly painted, and a necklace pattern in the front.

About one-fourth of the way up is a large rock about 50 feet in height, slightly arched toward the trail (Figs. 143 and 144). This was a special place, though its current neglect does not acknowledge that. It was the third "cemetery" discovered by Bingham's team, 1,000 feet above the Main Gate. Here they found the finest grave at Machu Picchu, labeled No. 26. Figure 145 is the floor plan of the Rock-sheltered Terrace and the location of Burial 26. Figure 146 shows a female skeleton in a contracted position with pottery and the skeleton of a small collie-like dog. George F. Eaton, Bingham's osteologist in charge of the burial sites, reported that the woman buried here was well provided with personal articles and pottery. These artifacts make the site remarkable: no gold or silver, but three very choice pieces of pottery, a concave bronze mirror, small bronze tweezers, bronze *tupus*, a dainty bronze curette with an ornamental head in the design of a flying bird, and other items. Figure 147 is a sketch of a pot published in the February, 1915, issue of *National Geographic* magazine. Although the caption does not state where it was found, a comparison with Figure 146 shows that it came from Burial 26. The pot is on display in the Machu Picchu exhibit at Yale University's Peabody Museum, when not on loan.

Then, about one-half of the way up, is a fine site that we considered a check station in the first edition of this book (Fig. 148). We also noted a shrine with a carved rock and other structures (Fig. 149). We also stated, "Here a broad granite stairway leads abruptly into the impenetrable forest, probably a connecting trail" (Fig. 150). Then in September, 2002, we decided to find out. Our team, made up of several Cusco University archaeologists and macheteros from Aguas Calientes, led by Ives Bejar and coauthors Valencia and Wright, explored the whole site and made some startling discoveries. At the top of the granite stairway, just a few feet into the thick forest, there was an entrance through a stone wall with four narrow steps (Fig. 151). Disappointingly, they did not lead to a trail. So we continued clearing the tangle of trees and brush in all directions. Finally below the stairs and to the left, a retaining wall on the upper (mountain) side was exposed.

Figure 148. Shrine and security station at juncture of two trails: the Inca Trail and a newly discovered side trail.

Figure 149. Carved stone shrine along the Inca Trail

Figure 150. Broad granite stairway leading into dense forest

Figure 151. At the top of the granite stairway, an entrance through a stone wall with four narrow steps

Then another retaining wall on the downhill side, and paving stones in between—the beginning of the sought-after trail (Fig 152). Painstakingly the team followed the clues, cutting through the jungle-like growth (Fig. 153), finding more walls, stone steps, rock falls with an intermittent loss of trail, all the way to the ridge of Machu Picchu Mountain. We designated it "Trail L" (Fig. 154). We surmise that the trail goes beyond the ridge to Intipata, an agricultural enclave where food stuffs for Machu Picchu would have been grown and brought in by llama trains. Another branch likely goes up to the summit of Machu Picchu Mountain. A den with a bear cub was noted—additional habitat for the rare and endangered Spectacled bear, as on the lower East Flank (Fig. 136, page 115). It should be noted that the trail was not cleared more than to identify and survey its location by GPS (Geographical Positioning System).

Figure 152. Measuring the width at the beginning of the trail

Figure 153. Clearing the tangle of trees and brush and finding a retaining wall of the sought-after trail

126

Figure 154. "Trail L" from Huaca 17 to Ridgeline is shown in white

But what of the four stone steps? They led to the discovery of an unusual semicircular platform, about 25 feet in length, formed by an Inca masonry wall about 4 feet high (Fig. 155). If more of the vegetation were removed, it would have an outstanding 180 degree view from Intipunko on the right, down to Machu Picchu and beyond on the left (Fig 156). It was undoubtedly a ceremonial platform, with a security control function. The fact that the main Inca Trail and the newly discovered trail from the ridge join at this complex adds to its significance. This site was much more than an ordinary check station. It was a final control point for two trails to Machu Picchu and had a ceremonial function for travelers on these trails. All of the structures of the complex have been meticulously recorded on a floor plan, "Huaca 17—Security Station on Inca Trail" (Fig 157). On the upper end is Huaca 17, a shrine (designated "A" on the floor plan) consisting of a large carved *in-situ* rock similar to the rock in the Temple of the Sun. Several wayronas face it, including the large one with the central column on the other side of the Inca Trail (B, C, D). Two additional buildings (E, H) have entrances that have been constructed in such a way as to make them private from the staircase. Then at the head of the wide granite staircase is the ceremonial platform—all combined to create an important religious site on the Inca Trail. Now more questions need to be answered, such as: are there any burials here like at the Rock-Sheltered Terrace with the overhanging rock? And since we know that the Inca did not build stairways without a purpose, where do the narrow steps between the pillars on the downhill (east) side of the complex lead to?

The final approach to Intipunku is steep, and there are small terraces in the gully to prevent erosion. If the trail has been hot, this is a good place to cool down with shade and a breeze. You can see the continuation of the Inca Trail down the other side. (The next stop is Wiñay Wayna, a beautiful *tambo* with a series of sixteen fountains. It is nearly a day's round-trip from Machu Picchu and is also described later in this section. If you have a day for Wiñay Wayna, you can simply incorporate that side trip with this one.) The return trip is a delight, with breathtaking views.

Figure 155. Semicircular platform, 25 feet long, 4 feet high, formed by an Inca masonry wall

Figure 156. View to Machu Picchu and beyond

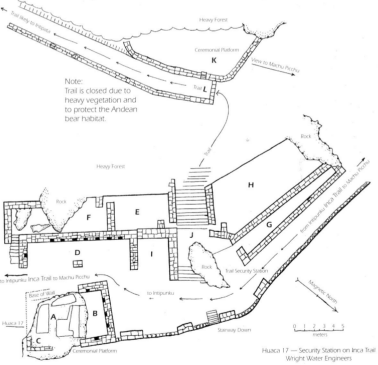

Trail likely to Intipata

Heavy Forest

Ceremonial Platform

K

View to Machu Picchu

Note:
Trail is closed due to
heavy vegetation and
to protect the Andean
bear habitat.

Trail L

Trail

Rock

Heavy Forest

H

from Intipunku Inca Trail to Machu Picchu

Rock

F

E

G

J

D

I

Rock

Trail Security Station

to Intipunku Inca Trail to Machu Picchu

Base of Wall

to Intipunku

Magnetic North

Huaca 17

A

B

0 1 2 3 4 5
meters

C

Ceremonial Platform

Stairway Down

Huaca 17 — Security Station on Inca Trail
Wright Water Engineers

Figure 157. Huaca 17—Security Station on Inca Trail

Huayna Picchu, including Uña Picchu and Alternate Trail to the Temple of the Moon

This remarkable mountain should be on your list of things to do at Machu Picchu if your schedule permits. As seen from a distance and in the classic photos, it just seems like a magnificent backdrop for Machu Picchu. On closer view you can see steep terraces hanging on the precipitous slopes and structures perched on cliffs (Fig. 158). This was a holy mountain, and as you shall see, intensely developed with stairs, tunnels, high status terraces, shrines, and other carvings and structures. It would have been

Figure 158. On Huayna Picchu, steep terraces hang on precipitous slopes and structures perch on cliffs

heavily used in Inca times, from noblemen surveying their main and performing ceremonies to their gods at the summ workers tending the plants on the terraces. It is still an insµ-- and breathtaking place. We recommend climbing Huayna Picchu, not only for the views, but also because of the wonderful ruins near the summit, some of which were under construction when the Inca workers stopped work and left. Our team of archaeologists, engineers, and Qechua Indians from Aguas Calientes examined, measured, and documented the structures, surveyed the site, and studied prehistoric crops grown on the terraces. We prepared the "Archaeological Map of the Summit of Huayna Picchu" (Fig. 159), which is meant to help you appreciate the spectacular work Inca civil engineers accomplished 500 years ago.

The climb looks more challenging than it really is, and almost anyone can get to the summit on a nice day. Plan to spend about one hour up and a half hour down, with at least three hours overall to more fully appreciate this holy mountain with the inspiring views. From below, the mountaintop looks inaccessible; however, the Inca constructed a well-defined and rather formalized trail to the very top. Granite stairways exist in many places (Fig. 160). For the modern visitors' convenience, a few railings and ropes have been added to provide an additional sense of security. Fascinating ruins appear along the upper portion of the trail. Be sure to linger at intermediate points for full appreciation of Inca workmanship (and to catch your breath). Stop and admire the impressive terraces along the way.

To climb Huayna Picchu you must sign in at the checkpoint building behind the Sacred Rock before 1:00 P.M. (13:00). The cut-off time is enforced for safety, so that you will not be on the mountain late in the day. Avoid climbing Huayna Picchu in the rain or just after a rain because the trail can become slippery in places, and a slip can be fatal. You cannot rely on the tree branches to break your fall. From the checkpoint, you can easily follow the trail as it heads for the saddle ridge, just beyond the smaller Uña Picchu, then goes in a generally northerly direction. (Note: there is a brief description of the trail to Uña Picchu at the end of this chapter.) When you reach the saddle, take a minute to examine the geology of the Huayna Picchu fault that runs right

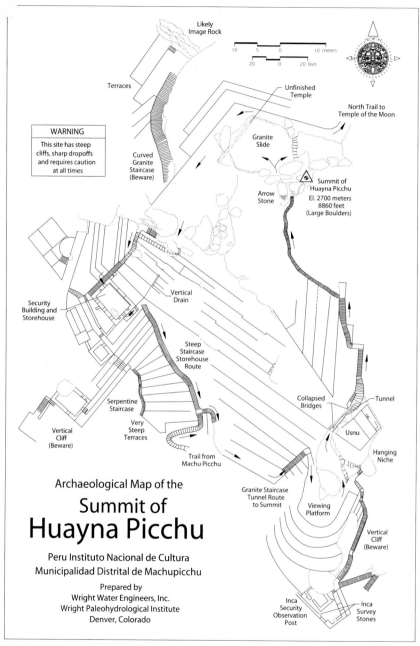

Figure 159. Archaeological Map of the Summit of Huayna Picchu

Figure 160. Steep stairway up to Huayna Picchu summit

next to where you are standing (see Fig. 11, page 12). About 10 minutes from the checkpoint, you will know that you have reached the start of the Huayna Picchu climb: the trail becomes steep, and your labored breathing will verify that you are on your way up the remarkable and beautiful mountain, that, even today, is revered by the Inca descendants. In some places the trail is rocky, in others the trail consists of dirt that can become slippery. Sometimes you will climb on granite stairways. Imagine the Inca on the same stairway: priests heading up to perform ceremonies at the summit and workers to care for the terraces.

The first 40 minutes of your hike to the summit represent the most physical work. You may feel as though you are doing an endless Stair Master workout (but with much better scenery than the gym at home). After this steep climb, though, you will arrive at a sharp right turn and your first view of the fine, high-level terraces. The trail forks when it is about 90 percent of the way to the summit to form a summit loop. Now find your location on the "Archaeological Map of the Summit of Huayna Picchu" so you can coordinate the rest of your climb on the map. At the fork in the trail, there is a long, steep stairway on the left

(Fig. 161). This is the storehouse route. To the right is the tunnel route. We recommend that you take the tunnel route. Go up the granite staircase and spend five or ten minutes at the viewing platform (Fig. 162) for one of the most spectacular scenic views in the Western Hemisphere (Fig. 2, page 2). Directly below is a security observation post on the edge of the cliff (Fig. 163). It is walled on three sides and has two large windows that enabled the Inca security personnel to observe the entire area below. You will see two long, upright rocks in the building, which suggest a sacred purpose. Looking to the left and down, you can see the thick rain forest of the lower east flank of Machu Picchu, with its ancient cliff-side terraces that are cleared from time to time. You may also see portions of the recently uncovered East Flank Inca Trail (Fig. 132, page 113), an extension of the main Inca Trail that led to the river below and the Vilcabamba region to the east.

While on the platform, turn around and look upwards; there you will see a collapsed bridge stone that connected the terraces on your left to the three-tiered structure above that is a holy *usnu*. Finally, walk over to the right where you can see a quadrangular ceremonial hanging niche cut into the vertical precipice that faces easterly. The Inca would have had to use some sort of scaffolding to cut this spectacular niche out of the sheer rock face (Fig. 164).

Figure 161. Long, steep stairway on the storehouse route to the summit of Huayna Picchu

Figure 162. Granite stairway and viewing platform on the tunnel route to the summit of Huayna Picchu

Figure 163. Security observation post directly below the viewing platform

Figure 164. Quadrangular ceremonial hanging niche cut into a vertical precipice

Now you are ready to go up a few stairs and through the tunnel with a staircase at the far end, where you will find it a tight squeeze if you are wearing a backpack (Fig. 165). Upon exiting the tunnel, keep going up the stairs for about 40 feet and turn around to get a good view of the important *usnu* (Fig. 166). Finding an *usnu* near the summit of Huayna Picchu is a stunning surprise. Usually in the main plaza of an Inca community, this small but significant structure was built as an elegantly raised platform, often stepped and in pyramidal shape, and used by the Inca for diverse purposes: an altar, a place of prayer and sacrifice, a throne and seat for the Inca, a place for the Inca or someone else who governed to hold court and dispense justice. It is said that the *usnu* was a symbol of the power and government of the Inca. This must be the most spectacular site for an *usnu* in the entire Inca empire, with the whole sacred center of Machu Picchu lying before it. For an additional view do not hesitate climbing onto the *usnu* if you have time, recognizing its significance in Inca

Figure 165. Tunnel steps cut into the granite of Huayna Picchu

Figure 166. Viewing an *usnu* near the summit of Huayna Picchu

Figure 166a. An Inca seated on an *usnu*

137

times. Note the fine stonework of the staircases ahead of you; they have endured without restoration since the time Machu Picchu was abandoned in the 16th century.

Next, after the long granite staircase, you will reach a jumble of huge boulders that you must climb under, around, and over to reach the summit (Fig. 167). Plan to spend enough time on the summit of the holy mountain of Huayna Picchu to examine its features. Note the huge, carved granite rock that has been shaped to form what looks like a seat (Fig. 168). The V-shaped carving is actually an arrow stone that points south to Mount Salcantay, another holy mountain 20 miles away. The arrow is similar to three arrow stones at various locations in Machu Picchu, all pointing south. Salcantay is often covered with clouds, but on a clear day you might see a small portion of its peak behind the far-off skyline.

The incomparable view from the summit reveals many Machu Picchu sites, such as the Intiwatana, the Temple of the Sun, the Sacred Rock, and the wonderful agricultural fields and green

Figure 167. You must climb under, around, and over boulders to reach the summit

Figure 168. An arrow stone points to Mount Salcantay, another holy mountain 20 miles away

plazas. Look for the Guardhouse in the distance and follow the Inca Trail as it slopes up to Intipunku. Look east to the peaks of the Mount Veronica Range and the ice cap on Mount Veronica. Then look west to the San Miguel Range. Behind you, the ridge seemingly plunges straight down to the Urubamba River that encircles the summit on three sides.

The Inca ruins on and near the summit provide ample evidence of the ceremonial nature of Huayna Picchu, particularly when coupled with the impressive Temple of the Moon on the north face of the mountain, which can be accessed by a very steep trail from the top of Huayna Picchu. That route is described at the end of this chapter. The usual route to the Temple of the Moon is directly from Machu Picchu and is described in "Side Trip: Temple of the Moon." The seemingly huge random rocks at the summit are reminiscent of the granite pinnacles of the Unfinished Temple south of the Sacred Rock.

Figure 169. This carved stone was in the process of being moved by workers when the place was abandoned

In 2002 we inspected the summit rocks and noted that the large rock just east of the arrow stone is partially shaped on its underside where it lies against the arrow stone (Fig. 169). This carved side of the stone is virtually inaccessible as it lies now, indicating that it had been in transit, that is, it was likely in the process of being moved by the workers when the place was abandoned. We believe that the summit of Huayna Picchu was to be further developed into some type of shrine-like structure.

After departing the summit, you will come to a huge, sloped granite slide rock that can be slippery when wet, so bypass it if you are unsure of your footing. There is a route that runs around the slide rock that can be used as an alternative to walking or sliding down the rock face. The sloped rock shows evidence of polishing. At its base, there is the beginning of a wall that has many carefully set stones, which would eventually have been another structure. Take your time there to note the fine work by the Inca stonemasons (Fig. 170).

You may want to check out the curved granite staircase to the northwest with views of the Urubamba River below, good ter-

Figure 170. The beginning of a wall that would eventually have been another structure

race stonework, and what may be image carving on the rocky ridge to the north, replicating the mountains in the background. However, do *not* go down the curved staircase if it is wet or you feel unsure of your footing. The staircase is partially crumbled at its beginning; a fall here could be fatal.

Your next stop is a two-story security building and storehouse that was restored in 2001 (Fig. 171). The lower floor has two doorways ideally sited for security and control of the summit. The southeast side has three windows that provide a spectacular panoramic view. The second floor would have been created with timbers and would have had a floor of compacted clay. Access to the second floor for storage goods was via a wide opening on the northeast side of the building. Look around and downward from the building to see marvelous feats of Inca engineering in the form of hanging terraces to the west and below (Fig. 172). Looking back to the storehouse from below is also a spectacular view (Fig. 173).

Figure 171. Two-story security building and storehouse that was restored in 2001

Figure 172. Hanging terraces below the storehouse

142

Figure 173. Looking back to the storehouse from below

We collected soil samples from two sets of terraces on the top of Huayna Picchu in 2002. It was expected that pollen laboratory testing would provide evidence of maize (corn). But to our surprise, no maize was found; instead there was abundant mate (pronounced matay). Mate is used for brewing an aromatic beverage that we know as Paraguayan tea with stimulant properties.

From the two-story building, look into the gully below where you will see the long, steep staircase that is your route home, the alternative to the tunnel on the way up (Fig. 174). Most people go down the staircase sitting and facing forward. One advantage

Figure 174. A long, steep staircase below the storehouse is the alternative to the tunnel route

Figure 175. Terraces on the steep slope to the right of the staircase

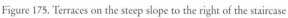

to facing forward is the opportunity to admire the fantastic terraces on your right and wonder how they ever could have been built on such a steep slope (Fig. 175). The stairway looks worse than it is — nevertheless, use caution. The return down to the checkpoint should take about one-half hour.

Alternate Route to the Temple of the Moon

The usual trail to the Temple of the Moon takes you directly from Machu Picchu around the north side of Huayna Picchu Mountain and is described in "Side Trips: Temple of the Moon." However, you can get to the temple directly from the top of Huayna Picchu Mountain. The trail from the summit of Huayna Picchu to the Temple of the Moon is typically hiked as a one-way route. The trail begins in the northeast summit area of Huayna Picchu and access is gained near the slide rock. To the east of the slide rock (actually behind the slide rock) is the trailhead for the little-traveled trail. The trail descends 1,250 feet (380 meters) over a distance of approximately 2,600 feet (0.8 kilometers), making for a very steep 48 percent average slope trail. The trail begins by following the northeast ridge of Huayna Picchu. This gentle trail soon gives way to a steep descent. At the start of the descent, you will encounter a narrow ledge passing below an overhanging rock wall. Fortunately, a steel cable has been installed along the face of this rock to hold on to as you cross this daunting portion of the trail. After navigating this ledge, you climb down a ladder (Fig. 176), moving onto a less precipitous, although still steep, portion of the trail. The trail is direct as it continues down to the Temple of the Moon, making for a quick access to the temple from the summit. From there you will be taking the usual route back to Machu Picchu, as described in "Side Trips: Temple of the Moon." Since this is one of the lesser-traveled trails at Machu Picchu, it is not as well maintained as some of the other routes. The jungle is consistently trying to encroach on the trail, and you must be careful not to trip over roots or slip on damp vegetation on the trail. Since it is likely that you will not encounter other hikers along this trail, you must not hike this trail alone.

Figure 176. A daunting portion of the trail to the Temple of the Moon

Trail to Uña Picchu

The trail to Uña Picchu is a short hike that is not often traveled by tourists, but it provides a wonderful and unique birds-eye view of Machu Picchu, especially the northern portion of the Urban Sector. This view is included in the first colored photo section. If you do not feel like going up Huayna Picchu, this could be an alternate choice. The trail spans a distance of about one-third mile (0.5 kilometers), with a net elevation gain of approximately 200 feet (60 meters) from the checkpoint behind the Sacred Rock to the summit of Uña Picchu. This easy hike begins by following the Huayna Picchu Trail, but quickly breaks off at an opening on the west side to lead up Uña Picchu. Since this trail is not extensively traveled, the branch trail to Uña Picchu is poorly marked. If you get to the first cabled portion of the Huayna Picchu Trail leading down to the saddle between Huayna Picchu and Uña Picchu, you have gone too far.

Just after you leave the main trail to Huayna Picchu and climb a short distance to the beginning of the terraces, you will see the remainder of a double-jamb doorway. Walk up to the saddle and look down at the Urubamba River far below and up to the west face of Huayna Picchu. Note the high status terraces around you. The summit of Uña Picchu is a short ten-minute scramble upwards along the Machu Picchu side of the steep ridge that leads to the summit. The summit of Uña Picchu provides excellent views of the Intiwatana and the Unfinished Temple.

Soil samples from the Uña Picchu terraces showed a total lack of maize, even though nearly all of the Machu Picchu terraces contained abundant maize pollen. Likely, the Uña Picchu terraces were used for growing herbs and flowers.

Temple of the Moon

The Temple of the Moon was not discovered by Hiram Bingham's team but is a more recent find, from 1936, lying 1,280 feet (390 meters) below the summit on the north side of Huayna Picchu. It consists of three structural components: an overhanging cave with superb stonework, a very tall double-jamb doorway beyond, and, farther beyond, several structures including one that again uses a cave. The name of this site is problematic; there is no indication that a lunar ritual played any part in the use of this shrine. It is likely that someone simply called it Temple of the Moon as a counterpart to the Temple of the Sun, and the name stuck.

Figure 177. Stairway to the Temple of the Moon; the temple was discovered in 1936 on the north side of Huayna Picchu

Figure 178. Temple of the Moon protected by a huge rock overhang

Figure 179. Tallest double-jamb doorway in Machu Picchu area; the double-jamb on the outside indicates a special place beyond

To get to the temple, start at the same sign-in booth for climbing Huayna Picchu and take the same trail. Again, there is a 1:00 P.M. (13:00) cutoff time. After a short hike, the trail splits, the one to the Temple of the Moon turning left. A sign indicates that the hike to the temple from that point takes about one hour. Generally the trail leads down, but there are many rises and drops, so that there are ups and down both coming and going (Fig. 177). Do not go down this trail if it is raining or if the trail is wet. It can become very muddy, and parts of the trail are steep and exposed. Even when it is dry, parts of the trail require that you step down sideways. But the hike is well worth it.

Here is an unusual temple built under a huge rock overhang, or cave, with particularly fine and smooth stonework (Fig. 178). No rooms were created here—just walls, recesses, and niches. Some of the niches are set off by flat triple-frames, the only ones of such design in the Machu Picchu area. There is also a large rock carved into a seat or "altar." Why such superb workmanship in a relatively remote location? Perhaps because the Inca

Figure 180. Additional structures beyond the Temple of the Moon, including a small walled-in cave with a doorway and windows

150

revered mountains and the gods that inhabited them. Caves, like springs, were thought to be entrances for the gods. Here is a very large cave on the slope of a holy mountain, Huayna Picchu, worthy of being used for worshipping the mountain and its gods.

Continue down the trail through a very tall double-jamb doorway (Fig. 179). Note that the double jamb is on the outside, that is, coming up from below it would signify a special place beyond. Farther down are additional structures (Fig. 180). One is a small cave that is walled in, with a doorway and windows, and also has much more crudely fashioned internal niches.

You can see that it was an important complex and could have been a destination for worship from Machu Picchu. It likely served as a shrine along a trail from the Urubamba River to Machu Picchu. The doorway with its double-jamb on the downslope side reinforces this theory. The lower part of the trail is inaccessible at present. On the return hike you will enjoy a new vista of Machu Picchu from the northeast.

Machu Picchu Mountain

To add some adventure to your Machu Picchu visit, and if you have time, you may want to invest about three to four hours in a climb to the summit of the holy Machu Picchu Mountain. The view from the top is superb (Fig. 181). Plan for about two hours up and one hour down. You should take some water, and a lunch is advisable. You can find the trailhead by referring to the fold-out map: start on the Inca Trail to Cusco, then take the staircase on the west side of the trail, roughly 500 feet (150 meters) up from the Guardhouse. The map shows an arrow to "Inca Trail to Machu Picchu Mountain."

Figure 181. The grand view from the top of Machu Picchu Mountain looking north. Machu Picchu lies on the ridge with Huayna Picchu dominating the background. The Urubamba River encircles the site on three sides

Figure 182. A fine granite stairway high on Machu Picchu Mountain, signifying its importance and holy status

The route from the trailhead is evident but, as soon as you enter the forest beyond the terrace, you might lose the trail; if you do, go back and try again. A little farther on, the trail built by the Inca is well defined. In fact, you will find that the trail has many portions made of granite stones and others with beautiful staircases.

As you hike upward you will see a cave that Hiram Bingham examined in 1912; an Inca stone quarry at the Machu Picchu fault that yielded the green serpentine rock that is used sparingly in Machu Picchu; and viewing platforms. Nearer to the summit lies a long, curved granite staircase (Fig. 182). While admiring it, you may wonder about the human energy the Inca used in building such a fine stairway so high up on the mountainside. At the summit there is a small building that Bingham described as a signal station; however, this was much more than a place to watch for intruders. This was the summit of a holy mountain that even today is a special place for the Quechua Indians. They even fly an "Inca Empire" flag here.

Be sure to take along plenty of film, because the summit views are spectacular! Down below are the encircling Urubamba River, the Aguas Calientes area, the regional geologic faults, and of course Machu Picchu itself. Look east to the rounded slab-like, holy Putucusi Mountain and to the snow-capped Mt. Veronica. To the west you can admire the San Miguel Range and, if you are lucky, you may be able to glimpse the summit of Salcantay Mountain to the south.

Investigate the terraces on the summit, and also the small cave. After reveling in the grandeur of the 360-degree views, you can begin your descent, which should take about one hour. Be sure to take the time to appreciate the grand views going down. When you return to the Inca Trail, look up the trail to Intipunku (Gate of the Sun) to get a feeling for the geography, and then look back at the summit of Machu Picchu Mountain, which is in full view.

Wiñay Wayna

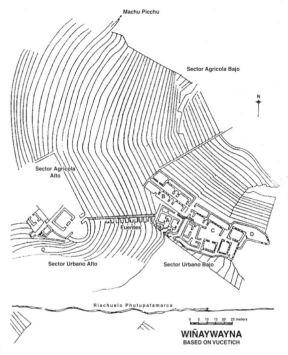

Figure 183. Map of Wiñay Wayna (Eternally Young), an excellent *tambo* (way station) for Pachacuti on his journey from Cusco

In 1942 Andean scholar Julio C. Tello named Wiñay Wayna (Eternally Young) after the orchid by the same name. The orchid (*Epidendrum secundum*) is found in the area between Machu Picchu and Wiñay Wayna. It is aptly named because Wiñay Wayna is a refreshing overnight stop along the Inca Trail, and from here it is only 5 miles (8 kilometers) to Machu Picchu. It was a *tambo* for the ruler Pachacuti on his journey from Cusco.

As you head for Wiñay Wayna up the Inca Trail from the Guardhouse in the early morning, you will see many fascinating ruins along the way. Except for a brief stop at Intipunku, keep going so as to reach Wiñay Wayna early enough for full enjoyment. Save the trailside ruins for the trip back.

Following a two to three hour walk from Machu Picchu and rounding the last curve in the trail, the site of Wiñay Wayna will suddenly spread out before you in all its glory. Note the upward sweep of the green mountain backdrop, the mountain creek waterfall, and the forty-one curved agricultural terraces that fit the hillside like a well-tailored glove (Figs. 184 and 185). Drink in the view in the midmorning sun or rainfall. Then, walk on a level contour across the expanse of terraces to the urban area and the great staircase, noting the high quality of the stone walls on your right.

Wiñay Wayna contains a northern agricultural sector and a southern urban area. The urban area has two parts: the upper to the west and the lower to the east. First explore the upper part, the area for visiting dignitaries, which contains four building enclosures, four fountains, and the incoming canal water supply. From the first building on the left, which is curved and has many windows, look out at the spectacular view and the lower urban sector. The buildings have the same structural features as at Machu Picchu. The walls are similarly tapered too, at about 5 degrees from vertical. The wall openings are mostly trapezoidal and vary in size. Note the barholds and receptacles for rounded roof beams. Imagine the inside walls being plastered and sometimes painted. Also note the special hydraulics of Wiñay Wayna throughout the site. There are drainage channels, small canals, drains, and depressions in the face of the walls and along the stairways.

In addition to the four fountains in the upper urban area, there is a series of eleven public fountains between the upper and lower urban sectors, each with a small entrance off the main stairway and a private fountain at the end. They are quadrangular and each has a stone-carved channel to direct the flow of water from the fountain into the stone basin below and a circular drain hole in the bottom. Some of the fountains have carved handholds for use when leaning forward to drink the jetting water. The Inca diverted the water from the nearby mountain creek. This diversion canal

Figure 184. Stone structures, forty-one terraces, and mountain creek waterfall of Wiñay Wayna

has been made to flow again after four hundred fifty years, adding its own magic to the site.

The lower urban sector is a masterpiece of layout with a long stone bench, and a double-jamb doorway with barholds and a ring at the top, similar to the doorway to Conjunto 2 at Machu Picchu. Do not miss the unique window at the far end of the sector, which was specially designed for a perfect view of the waterfall. Wiñay Wayna was a good place to live, work, and stop for a respite. When heading back, pause for a last view of Wiñay Wayna before rounding the corner beyond the terraces.

On the trail back to Machu Picchu you will want to examine the *wayrona* on the left side of the trail with its magnificent view of the distant peaks. Note the steep cliffs with two log bridges for the trail. After climbing a steep staircase about two-thirds of the way back, note the defensive stations for controling Inca Trail traffic. Then, of course, be sure to stop at Intipunku to see Machu Picchu spread out below, about 1¼ miles (a little more

Figure 185. Wiñay Wayna waterfall

than 2 kilometers) away. (See "Side Trip: Intipunku [Gate of the Sun].") There are several interesting structures between Intipunku and Machu Picchu that are well worth your time. Finally, as you make your way down to Machu Picchu, examine the stonework of the trail itself. This is the Inca Trail!

The Birds of Machu Picchu

By Gary Graham, Executive Director of Colorado Audubon

The beautiful and unique birds seen and heard throughout Machu Picchu explain why the area is becoming a spectacular and popular destination for birdwatchers and other nature tourists. Peru is one of the most biologically diverse countries in the world due in part to its tropical location and the tremendous variation in habitats. This unique country, with at least 1,800 species of birds, has more than half the number found throughout South America and double the number of birds recognized for North America. Over 400 species are recorded in a new book, *Field Guide to the Birds of Machu Picchu, Peru,* from the large protected sanctuary surrounding the ruins.

There are four major habitats around the Machu Picchu ruins: river, cloud forest, secondary forest growth, and open areas. You will see some of the most unique birds in the forests and along the river near Aguas Calientes before and after you ascend to the ruins. Watch for Mitred Parakeets, Torrent Ducks, Torrent Tyrannulets (small flycatchers), Andean Gulls and White-capped Dippers above, along, or in the river. Mixed flocks of colorful tanagers, sometimes accompanied by Ocellated Piculets, a small woodpecker, dart and forage in the canopy of the tall forests at lower elevations. Be sure to look for brilliant hummingbirds like the Gould's Inca, the energetic Bananaquit, and the strikingly beautiful Blue-necked Tanager at the edge of the forest near some of the hotels and along the railroad tracks. One of the birding treasures of Machu Picchu is an area, called a lek, about a kilometer below the railroad station where up to a dozen large, orange and black males of the national bird of Peru, the Andean

Cock-of-the-Rock fly, call rowdily, and put on colorful displays to attract females.

The tall forest, referred to by scientists as the pre-montane forest, transitions at higher elevations to the humid montane forest, which is denser and shorter in stature. Along ridge tops this forest becomes a stunted, almost impenetrable habitat known by some as the elfin forest. Birds are harder to see in these forests but look for tanagers, such as the amazing Scarlet-bellied Mountain-Tanager, and hummingbirds foraging around the edges and near the many canopy-dwelling flowers that characterize this zone. Also, listen for the beautiful, sometimes melancholic, songs of the forest interior species such as the Red-and-white Antpitta.

Although there is little native habitat within the ruins, you will see birds there. Search the secondary growth, gardens, and forest edges for a beautiful hummingbird called the Green Violetear, Rust-and-yellow Tanagers, Spectacled Whitestarts, White-winged Black-Tyrants, and Rusty Flowerpiercer, a remarkable little bird that robs nectar from flowers through a small hole it tears near flower's base. Listen for the ubiquitous song coming from the bamboo thickets of the Inca Wren, a species only recently described as new to science and found only in this region of Peru. White-tipped Swifts, Blue-and-white Swallows, which nest in the ruin walls, Chiguanco Thrushes, and Rufuous-collared sparrows are common in the open areas. Periodically search the sky and mountain ridges for the familiar Peregrine Falcon, as well as the chunky Black-chested Buzzard-Eagle, and the famous Andean Condor soaring occasionally high above the ruins.

An early morning walk up the Inca Trail to Wiñay Wayna through Intipunku from the ruins provides incredible views and fascinating birds. As you pass through the elfin forest and grassland patches enjoying the tanagers and hummingbirds, look and listen carefully for the Trilling Tapaculo, a small bird that sneaks around the understory more like a mouse, then surprises you with its long, loud song. Listen also for the Undulated Antpitta with its Screech Owl-like song and the Golden-headed Quetzal, an exceptionally attractive large, metallic green bird that is heard more often than seen. Finally, watch for the Amethyst-throated Sunangel, a small hummingbird with a descriptive name, and the enigmatic Giant Hummingbird. This, the largest hummingbird in the world, hovers like other hummingbirds, except you can see the wing beats, then glides away like a swallow.

We hope that we have whetted your appetite for bird watching at Machu Picchu. The *Field Guide to the Birds of Machu Picchu*, written in English by Barry Walker and illustrated by Jon Fjeldsa, is generously and beautifully illustrated with colored paintings of each bird, and is a wonderful addition to any library. The field guide can be obtained from:

1) <u>South American Explorer</u>. We are fortunate that the South American Explorer, with a headquarters office in New Jersey and clubhouses in Cusco and Lima, Peru, have the field guide for sale. WARNING: You need to let them know well in advance so it is available when you want it! The price is about $32 and a few dollars for shipping.

   a) South American Explorer, 126 Indian Creek Road, Ithaca, N.Y. 14850 USA
   Phone (607) 277-0488
   Fax (607) 277-6122
   explorer@saexplorers.org
   Website: http://www.saexplorers.org

   b) South American Explorer Lima Clubhouse. You can pick up the book directly at the Lima clubhouse, Calle Piura 135, Miraflores, Lima, Peru.
   Phone/Fax: (511) 445-3306
   limaclub@saexplorers.org

   c) South American Explorer Cusco Clubhouse. You can pick up the book directly from the Cusco clubhouse. Choquechaca 188, No.4, Cusco, Peru.
   Phone/Fax (51 84) 245-484
   cuscoclub@saexplorers.org

NOTE: We found that e-mail is the most efficient method of communicating with Peru. If you are ordering from the Lima or Cusco Clubhouses, make sure that they will be open when you want to pick up your book. We found that the Cusco Clubhouse is sometimes closed on the weekend.

2) Pick up directly from the publisher PROFONANPE in Lima (Miraflores) for $25. But they are in the process of moving at the time of this publication. Telephone and Fax and e-mail are staying the same.
   Tel: (00 51 1) 212 10 10; Fax: (00 51 1) 212 19 57
   e-mail: prf@profonanpe.org.pe

The book can be ordered for shipping at the e-mail address, but delivery to the US will cost a total of about $50 since they send it by courier.

Acknowledgments

Anyone who seriously studies Machu Picchu must start with Hiram Bingham, history professor and explorer. His outstanding photographs and writings provide documentation of the site as it existed in 1912. We are grateful to Yale University and the National Geographic Society for sponsoring Bingham's expeditions 1912–1915.

The Instituto National de Cultura, Cusco Region, its managers and staff, are most appreciated. It was the INC that assisted and encouraged us over a six-year period with advice, maps, and numerous documents. In particular, anthropologist Arminda Gibaja Oviedo generously gave us help and advice. The INC gave us permits to work in "off-limit" areas, such as the lower eastern flank, where we were able to discover and map a major Inca trail, fountains, and terraces. In addition, the elected officials of the Municipal District of Machu Picchu have been most cordial and helpful. On-site at Machu Picchu we appreciated the assistance of the INC staff and the workers from Aguas Calientes, many of whom were Chechua Indians and descendants of the Inca. No job was too big, too small, or too arduous. There were always willing hands. In particular we want to mention Pedro Ortiz, who helped us regularly from 1994 to the present.

We also thank Professor John Rowe and Research Associate Patricia Lyons of the University of California at Berkeley, and Professor Gordon McEwan of Wagner College for their encouragement and support of our investigations, together with their advice and assistance to ensure scientific and practical integrity of this book. Janet Schoeberlein translated the Valencia/Gibaja archaeological summary book into English, greatly facilitating communication between the coauthors.

Dr. Richard Burger and Lucy Salazar Burger of the Yale Peabody Museum were very cooperative and encouraging with scientific data as they prepared for the Machu Picchu Exhibit at Yale in 2003, designed to showcase the Bingham treasures.

We wish to thank the Rector and Assistant Rector of the Universidad Nacional de San Antonio Abad del Cusco for allowing Professor Alfredo Valencia to spend time and energy on our Machu Picchu projects, and making the scientific and library resources of the university freely available. Anthropologist Ives Bejar Mendoza was particularly valuable during our explorations and documentations of new findings.

National Geographic Research Cartographer Patricia Healy and artist Robert Guisti gave us permission to use the beautiful painting of Machu Picchu as it looked in Inca times. This was a major addition to this revised edition and is greatly appreciated. Another outside contributor was Gary Graham, describing the birds at Machu Picchu.

The authors also thank Wright Water Engineers of Denver for their technical and financial assistance since 1994 with exploration, mapping, surveying, graphics, and photographs for this book. In particular, Patti Pinson, Gary Witt, and Kurt Loptien were truly invaluable, as were Eric Bikis and Andrew Earles (who also wrote the Uña Picchu and alternate Temple of the Moon trails descriptions), Chris Crowley, Scott Marshall, and Jonathan Kelly. Finally we must acknowledge Kenneth Wright, who organized and led all of our field trips and wrote the chapters on the side trips to Huayna Picchu Mountain, Machu Picchu Mountain, and Winay Wayna.

Figure Credits

Ten figures by Hiram Bingham and his team were incorporated into the book. Figure 1 is from *National Geographic Magazine*, April 1913, and Figures 51 and 147 are from the February 1915 issue. Figures 16, 27, 44, 89, and 130 are from Hiram Bingham's 1930 book, *Machu Picchu: A Citadel of the Incas*. Finally, Figures 145 and 146 are from George F. Eaton's 1915 publication, "The Collection of Osteological Material from Machu Picchu."

Seven historic sketches by Huaman Poma de Ayala, published in 1614, (Figures on pp. xvii and xviii, and Figures 17, 43, 124, 126, and 166a), were provided by Dr. Gordon McEwan of Wagner College, Staten Island, NY, who photographed the sketches while Curator at the Dumbarton Oaks Museum.

The aerial photograph of Machu Picchu, by the U.S. Air Force in July 1963, was provided by Wright Water Engineers, Inc., Denver.

Vincent Lee, a Wyoming architect and Andean explorer, provided Figure 74.

Figure 136 was obtained from the World Wide Web.

The balance of the figures are credited to the following members of the Wright Paleohydrological Institute team who visited and worked at Machu Picchu at various times since 1994:

Will Allender: Figures 184 and 185.

Andres Earles, Hydraulic Engineer, Wright Water Engineers, Inc.: Figures 161, 162, 164, 166, 168, 171, 173, 174, and 176.

Julia M. Johnson, professional photographer with Peaks and Places Photography of Boulder and Vail, Colorado: Figures 10, 25, 28, 30, 31, 48, 80, 91, 124, 178, 179, and 180.

Kurt Loptien, Graphics Designer, Wright Water Engineers, Inc.: Figures 5, 11, 14, 19, 36, 39, 45, 52, 61, 71, 79, 82, 86, 97, 99, 101, 105, and 129.

Grosvenor Merle-Smith, photographer and Co-master and Huntsman of the Bull Run Hunt, Virginia: Figures 2, 3, 4, 7, 20, 29, 33, 50, 83, 85, 94, 100, 108, 110, 122, 123, 138, 139, and 144.

Kenneth R. Wright, President of Wright Water Engineers, Inc. and the Wright Paleohydrological Institute: Figures 6, 24, 26, 49, 53, 54, 77, 81, 102, 103, 112, 113, 117, 121, 125, 127, 128, 131, 132, 133, 134, 135, 151, 152, 153, 156, 158, 160, 163, 165, 167, 169, 170, 172, 175, 181, and 182.

Ruth M. Wright, Coauthor: Figures 8, 9, 13, 15, 18, 21, 22, 23, 32, 34, 35, 37, 38, 40, 41, 42, 46, 47, 55, 56, 57, 58, 59, 60, 62, 63, 64, 65, 66, 67, 68, 69, 70, 72, 74, 75, 76, 78, 84, 87, 88, 90, 92, 93, 95, 96, 98, 106, 107, 109, 111, 114, 115, 116, 118, 119, 120, 137, 140, 141, 142, 143, 148, 149, 150, 154, 155, and 177.

Wright Water Engineers, Inc. staff: Figures 157 and 159.

Alfredo Valencia Zegarra, Coauthor: Figures 73 and 183.

Glossary

aclla	Chosen women, whom the Spaniards called Virgins of the Sun.
aryballo	Pottery bottle for liquids.
ayllu	Kinship group.
ceques	Imaginary lines radiating from the center of Cusco to various sacred places.
chasqui	Inca messengers, who often ran in relays.
chicha	Maize beer, often used in ceremonies.
conjunto	A group of buildings, often surrounded by a wall, usually with a common purpose.
cuye	Guinea pig.
hanan	A physical and social division of many Inca towns, *hanan* being the higher, *hurin* the lower.
huaca	A holy place or sacred object.
hurin	See *hanan.*
intiwatana	The place to which the sun is tied.
kallanka	A great hall, with many entrances.
kancha	A walled habitation compound.
kero	Drinking cup.
machetero	A man whose working tool is the machete.
mita	Taxation in labor.
panaqa	Royal corporate family group.
qolqa	Storehouse.
quipu	A complex system of knotted cords used primarily for accounting.
tambo	Way station, inn.
tupu	A stickpin used to fasten a woman's cape or dress; also her principal item of jewelry.
usnu	A small but significant structure often stepped and in pyramidal shape, used for diverse purposes: a throne and seat for the Inca, or other authority figure, to hold court and dispense justice; also an altar, a place for prayer and sacrifice; a symbol of power and government.
wayrona	Three-sided rectangular building with one long side open, with a shed roof.

References

Bingham, Hiram. 1913. "In the Wonderland of Peru." *National Geographic Magazine,* April 23, 387–574.

———— 1930. *Machu Picchu: A Citadel of the Incas.* New Haven, CT: Yale University Press.

Burger, Richard L., and Lucy Salazar Burger. 1993. "Machu Picchu Rediscovered: The Royal Estate in the Cloud Forest." *Discovery* 24(2).

Dearborn, D. S., and R. E. White. 1982. "Archaeoastronomy at Machu Picchu." *Annals.* New York Academy of Sciences.

Dearborn, D. S. P., and R. E. White. 1983. "The 'Torreon' of Machu Picchu as an Observatory." *Archaeoastronomy* 5 (Journal for the History of Astronomy, xiv).

Dearborn, David S. P., Katharina J. Schreiber, and Raymond E. White. 1987. "Intimachay: A December Soltice Observatory at Machu Picchu, Peru." *American Antiquity* 52(2): 346–352.

Eaton, George F. 1916. "The Collection of Osteological Material from Machu Picchu." *Memoirs of the Connecticut Academy of Art and Sciences* 5, (May). New Haven.

Fejos, Paul. 1944. Archaeological Explorations in the Cordillera Vilcabamba. New York.

Frost, Peter. 1999. *Exploring Cusco: The Essential Guide to Peru's Most Famous Region.* 5th ed. Lima, Peru: Nuevas Imagenes.

Guaman Poma de Ayala, Felipe. 1978. *Letter to a King.* New York: E. P. Dutton. (Originally entitled *Nueva Coronica y Buen Gobierno,* written and illustrated before 1615.)

Lee, Vincent R. 1988. *"The Lost Half of Inca Architecture."* Paper presented to the Annual Meeting of the Institute of Andean Studies in Berkeley, California, January 8, 1988. P.O. Box 107, Wilson, WY 83014.

National Geographic Magazine. May 2002. Map supplement. "The Inca, Machu Picchu Salutes the Sun."

Protzen, Jean-Pierre. 1993. *Inca Architecture and Construction at Ollantaytambo*. New York: Oxford University Press.

Reinhard, Johan. 1991. *Machu Picchu: The Sacred Center*. Lima, Peru: Nuevas Imagines.

Rowe, John H. 1979. "An Account of the Shrines of Ancient Cuzco." *Nawpa Pacha*, 17. Berkeley, California, Institute of Andean Studies.

——— 1990. "Machu Picchu a la luz de documentos de siglo XVI." *Historica* 16(1): 139–154. (Machu Picchu in the light of documents of the sixteenth century)

——— 1997. Personal correspondence to the author, January.

Time-Life Books. 1992. *Incas: Lords of Gold and Glory*. Lost Civilizations Series. Alexandria, VA: Time-Life Books

Valencia Zegarra, A. 1977. *Excavaciones arqueologicas en Machupijchu: Sector de la "Roca Sagrada."* Cusco, Peru: Instituto Nacional de Cultura.

——— 1998. *Excavations on the Fountains of the East Flank of Machu Picchu*. Report prepared for Instituto Nacional de Cultura of Cusco.

Valencia Zegarra, Alfredo, and Arminda Gibaja Oviedo. 1992. *Machu Picchu: La investigacion y conservacion del monumento arqueologico despues de Hiram Bingham*. Cusco, Peru: Municipalidad del Qosqo.

Walker, Barry. 2002. *Field Guide to the Birds of Machu Picchu, Peru*. Lima, Peru: National Trust Fund for Natural Protected Areas.

Wright, K. R. 1996. "The Unseen Machu Picchu: A Study by Modern Engineers." *South American Explorer* 46(winter): 4–16.

Wright, K. R. and R. M. Wright. 1997. *Machu Picchu: Its Engineering Infrastructure*. The Institute of Andean Studies, 37th Annual Meeting, Berkeley, California, January 10. Revised February 3, 1997.

Wright, K. R., and A. Valencia Zegarra. 2000. *Machu Picchu: A Civil Engineering Marvel*. Reston, VA: ASCE Press.

Wright, K. R., J. M. Kelly, and A. Valencia Zegarra. 1997. "Machu Picchu: Ancient Hydraulic Engineering." *Journal of Hydraulic Engineering* 123(10): 838–843.

Wright, K. R., G. D. Witt, and A. Valencia Zegarra. 1997. "Hydrogeology and Paleohydrology of Ancient Machu Picchu." *Groundwater* 35(4): 660–666.

Wright, K. R., R. M. Wright, M. E. Jensen, and A. Valencia Zegarra. 1997. "Machu Picchu Ancient Agricultural Potential." *Applied Engineering in Agriculture* 132(1): 39–47.

Wright, K. R., A. Valencia Zegarra, and C. Crowley. 2000. "Archaeological Exploration of the Inca Trail, East Flank of Machu Picchu and Palynology of Terraces. Completion Report, Institute de Cultura." Denver: Wright Water Engineers and Wright Paleohydrological Institute. (Note: the results of the pollen testing by Linda Scott Cummings are included in this report)

Wright, K. R., A. Valencia Zegarra, and W. L. Lorah. 1999. "Ancient Machu Picchu Drainage Engineering." *Journal of Irrigation and Drainage Engineering*, Nov.–Dec.

Suggested Reading

Bingham, Hiram. 1913. "In the Wonderland of Peru." *National Geographic*, April 23, 387–574. The edition that stunned the world. Should be available in libraries or on the Web.

——— 1930. *Machu Picchu: A Citadel of the Incas*. New Haven, CT: Yale University Press. This is the bible by the man who rediscovered Machu Picchu for the modern world. Reissued 1979 by Hacker Art Books, Inc., New York.

Burger, Richard L., and Lucy Salazar Burger. 1993. "Machu Picchu Rediscovered: The Royal Estate in the Cloud Forest." *Discovery* 24(2). Six pages packed with new information and interpretations of the early discoveries by the Curator of Anthropology at Yale's Peabody Museum.

Frost, Peter. 1999. *Exploring Cusco: The Essential Guide to Peru's Most Famous Region*. 5th ed. Lima, Peru: Nuevas Imagenes. If you have not found the book elsewhere, this should be your first purchase upon arriving in Cusco. Small, popular (5th edition), well written, packed with information about sites, history, touring, hiking the Inca Trail, and much more.

Protzen, Jean Pierre. 1993. *Inca Architecture and Construction at Ollantaytambo*. New York: Oxford University Press. A great analysis of Inca architecture, planning, and construction, also applied to Machu Picchu. Many illustrations.

Reinhard, Johan. 1991. *Machu Picchu: The Sacred Center*. Lima, Peru: Nuevas Imagenes. The discoverer of the famous mummified Inca Maiden atop one of Peru's highest peaks, Reinhard presents a new perspective on Machu Picchu as it relates to sacred geography and its unique setting among the great mountains.

Saunders, Nicholas J. 2000. *The Incas*. Sutton Pocket Histories. Gloustershire, U.K.: Sutton Publishing Limited. A concise introduction to Inca history, religion, culture, creation of the empire, and the Spanish Conquest—all in 106 pages. New and inexpensive.

Time-Life Books. 1992. *Incas: Lords of Gold and Glory*. Lost Civilization Series. Alexandria, VA: Time-Life Books. Beautifully illustrated, including full-page color photographs, it covers history, art, crafts, textiles, mummies, Machu Picchu, and other sites. Try to find this book; it's a keeper.

Walker, Barry. 2002. *Field Guide to the Birds of Machu Picchu, Peru*. Lima, Peru: National Trust Fund for Natural Protected Areas.

Wright, K. R., and A. Valencia Zegarra. 2000. *Machu Picchu: A Civil Engineering Marvel*. Reston, VA: ASCE Press. Bingham said the "Incas were good engineers." This book proves it, and much more: remarkable city planning, infrastructure, water handling, types of walls and construction. Many beautiful black-and-white illustrations.

Index

Page numbers in **bold** indicate illustrations.

National Geographic
    magazine, *xiii*, 1, 106, 122
Niches
    in fountains, **23**, 24, 110
    framed, 150
    function of, 38, 46, **88**, 103
    as handholds, **88**, 89
    hanging, **132** (map), 134, **136**
    on Huayna Picchu, 134, **136**
    in "most beautiful wall," **26**
    mummies in, 103
    in Principal Temple, 46
    remodeled, 45, **48**
    in Royal Mausoleum, **28**
    in Sacristy, 50
    in Temple of the Condor, 93
    in Temple of the Sun, **26**, **28**
    trapezoidal shape of, 24
    "Unusual Niches Group," **89**
Nutritional analysis (of
    skeletons), 104

Observatory
    Inca technique for, 55–56
    at Intimachay (Cave of the
        Sun), 84, **85**, 86
    for solstice, 22, 84–86
    Temple of the Sun as, 22, 25
    See also Astronomical
        observations
Offerings, 65, 95, 116
Ollantaytambo
    Indian removal to, 105
    restoration at, 38
    travel options to, *viii*
Orchid (*Edidendrum
    secundum*), 155

Pachacuti (Inca ruler), *xv*, 155
    Machu Picchu and, 1
    Royal Residence and, 35
    in war regalia, *xvii*

Pacha Mama (earth goddess),
    115, 116
Paint (on walls), 76
Panaca, (panaqa)(royal
    corporate family group),
    1, 105, 167
Paraguayan tea, 143
Pegs
    pink granite, 47–48
    purpose of, 38
    in Temple of the Sun, 25,
        26
Peripheral Area C, 63
Peripheral Area F (side trip
    from), 117
Petroglyphs
    radiating lines, 63, **64**, 65
    Serpent Rock, **41**
Photography tips, *x*
Piccho, 1
Pins (*tupus*), **38**, 39, 122, 167
Pisac (site), 45, 55–56
Pizarro (conquistador), 95
Plaster (wall), 38, 47
Plazas
    function of, 10
    stone chips beneath, 43,
        111
    in Urban Sector, 5
Plumb bob (silver), **42**
Pollen analysis, 101, 143, 147
Population
    as elite, 10, 105
    estimates, 101, 105
Poroy (railroad station), *viii*
Pottery
    aryballos (bottles), 24, **109**,
        116, 167
    burial, **122**
    ceremonial breakage of, 45
    household and ceremonial,
        39

About the Authors

Ruth M. Wright wove a thirty-year fascination with Machu Picchu into an authorized investigation when she and her husband, Ken Wright of Wright Water Engineers, were granted a permit in 1994 from the Instituto Nacional de Cultura de Peru to conduct ongoing studies of the site. They live in Boulder.

Alfredo Valencia Zegarra is a professor in the Department of Anthropology and Archaeology at the University of Cusco and a registered professional archaeologist with the Instituto Nacional de Cultura de Peru. He spent several years as the resident archaeologist at Machu Picchu.

Archaeological Map of

Machu Picchu

Peru Instituto Nacional de Cultura

Prepared by
Machu Picchu Paleohydrological Survey
Wright Water Engineers, Inc.
Denver, Colorado USA

Paleohydrological Survey Team

Director and Paleohydrologist
Kenneth R. Wright

Assistant Director
Ruth M. Wright

Anthropologists
Dr. Alfredo Valencia Zegarra
Ives Bejar Mendoza

Archaeological Consultant
Dr. Gordon F. McEwan

Cartographers
Kurt A. Loptien
William S. Allender

Hydrogeologists
Gary D. Witt
Eric Bikis

Hydraulic Engineers
Jonathan M. Kelly
Andrew Earles

Librarian/Research Assistant
Patricia A. Pinson

Team Members
Grosvenor Merle-Smith
William L. Lorah
William Schoeberlein
Janet Schoeberlein
David Baysinger
Rita Lavato Baysinger
Julie Johnson

Map Sources

1. "Machu Picchu, A Citadel of the Incas," by Hiram Bingham, National Geographic Society, Yale University Press, 1930.

2. "Proyecto Senalizacion, Conjunto Arqueologico de Machu Picchu," 1987, Peruvian National Institute of Culture, 1:5000 scale plan.

3. "Plano de la Ciudadela Inca de Machu Picchu," 1966, Peruvian Tourism Corporation, 1:500 scale plan.

4. "Machu Picchu: La Investigacion y Conservacion del Monumento Arqueologico Despues de Hiram Bingham," Alfredo Valencia Zegarra and Arminda Gibaja Oviedo, 1992, Municipalidad del Qosqo.

5. Proprietary Field Surveys and Observations by Wright Water Engineers, Inc., 1994 to 1999.

Wright Water Engineers, Inc.
2490 West 26th Avenue, Suite 100A
Denver, Colorado 80211
(303) 480-1700

WRIGHT PALEOHYDROLOGICAL INSTITUTE

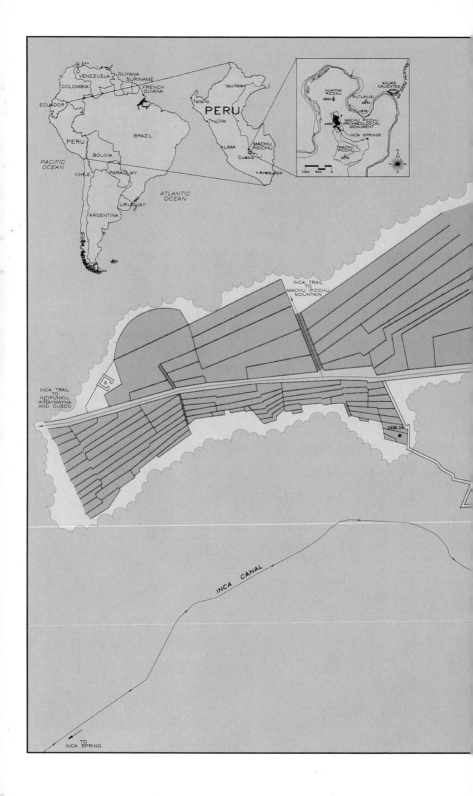

PERU

VENEZUELA GUYANA SURINAME
COLOMBIA FRENCH GUIANA
ECUADOR
PERU BRAZIL
BOLIVIA
PACIFIC OCEAN
CHILE PARAGUAY
ATLANTIC OCEAN
URUGUAY
ARGENTINA

Iquitos
Talara
Trujillo
LIMA
Cusco
MACHU PICCHU
Arequipa

HUAYNA PICCHU 2650
PUTUKUSI 2560
AGUAS CALIENTES 2050
1875
2450
MACHU PICCHU ARCHAEOLOGICAL MONUMENT
INCA SPRINGS
MACHU PICCHU 2575
RIO URUBAMBA
1000 500 0

INCA TRAIL TO MACHU PICCHU MOUNTAIN

INCA TRAIL TO INTIPUNKU, WIÑAYWAYNA AND CUSCO

2496.04

INCA CANAL

TO INCA SPRING

Archaeological Map of

Machu Picchu

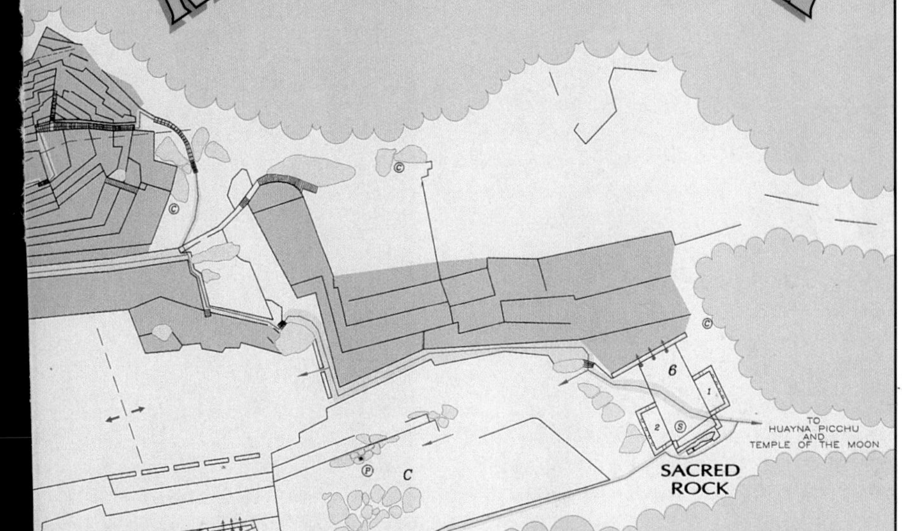

TO HUAYNA PICCHU AND TEMPLE OF THE MOON
SACRED ROCK
C
D
6
7
8
9
10
MAP LEGEND
SHRINE
TEMPLE
OBSERVATORY
PETROGLYPH
SUBTERRANEAN CAVE
TOURIST ROUTE
PRINCIPAL INCA ROUTE
STRUCTURAL WALLS WITH DOORWAYS, WINDOWS AND NICHES
DOUBLE JAMB DOORWAY
STONE ARROW POINTING SOUTH TO MT. SALCANTAY
ROCK OUTCROP
STAIRS
FOUNTAIN
MORTAR
1–18 CONJUNTO NUMBERS
2 ROOM NUMBER
ROOFLESS AREA
A–F PERIPHERAL AREAS
AGRICULTURAL AREA
CORRAL
INCA CANAL
DRAINAGE ROUTE
DRAINAGE OUTLET
DRAINAGE DIVIDE
2425.73 BENCHMARK
2000 KENNETH R. WRIGHT

Artist Robert Guisti's rendition of Machu Picchu as it appeared on the June 21 solstice celebration in the year 1530 at the height of the Inca Empire.

The art first appeared in the May 2002 map supplement of *National Geographic* magazine, and the magazine and artist Robert Guisti generously gave us permission to publish it here.

Ken Wright and coauthors Ruth Wright and Alfredo Valencia Zegarra were consultants to *National Geographic*, and one of our photographs was used as the basis for the painting.

ROCK
QUARRY

2447.47

B

SERPENT
ROCK

4

SACRED
PLAZA

INTIWATANA

2453.52

2450.91

WESTERN
URBAN SECTOR

PLAZA

3

GARDEN

EASTERN
URBAN SECTOR

18

18

17

16

16

15

14

13

SLIDE
2425.75

INTIMACHAY

9

12

13

18

N
W

S

E

NORTH

20 10 5 0   50 METERS

60 40 20 0   100 FEET

INCA TRAIL
TO
URUBAMBA RIVE

INCA TRAIL
TO
DRAWBRIDGE

F

TERRACE
OF THE
CEREMONIAL
ROCK

2499.86

UPPER
AGRICULTURAL
SECTOR

GUARDHOUSE

TRAIL FROM CUSCO

TRAIL TO GUARDHOUSE

MAIN
GATE

DRY MOAT

INCA CANAL

UNFINISHED CANAL

CITY WALL

A

LOWER
AGRICULTURAL
SECTOR

TRAIL TO GUARDHOUSE

TO
TOURIST HOTEL

E

2422.74

50   40   30

100   80